¶·B The Practitioner's Bookshelf

Hands-On Literacy Books for
Classroom Teachers and Administrators

Dorothy S. Strickland, Celia Genishi, and Donna E. Alvermann
LANGUAGE AND LITERACY SERIES EDITORS*

Literacy Leadership in Early Childhood:
The Essential Guide

Dorothy S. Strickland and Shannon Riley-Ayers

* For a list of current titles in the Language and Literacy Series, see *www.tcpress.com*

Literacy Leadership in Early Childhood

THE ESSENTIAL GUIDE

DOROTHY S. STRICKLAND
SHANNON RILEY-AYERS

Foreword by Barbara T. Bowman

Teachers College
Columbia University
New York and London

National Association
for the Education of
Young Children

Published simultaneously by Teachers College Press, 1234 Amsterdam Avenue, New York, NY 10027 and the National Association for the Education of Young Children, 1313 L Street NW, Suite 500, Washington, DC 20005

Library of Congress Cataloging-in-Publication Data

Strickland, Dorothy S.
    Literacy leadership in early childhood : the essential guide / Dorothy S. Strickland and Shannon Riley-Ayers.
    p. cm. — (Language and literacy series. Practitioner's bookshelf)
    Includes bibliographical references and index.
    ISBN 978-0-8077-4772-8 (pbk. : alk. paper)
    1. Language arts (Early childhood)—United States. I. Riley-Ayers, Shannon. II. Title.
    LB1139.5.L35S97 2007
    372.6—dc22   2006103048

ISBN 978-0-8077-4772-8 (paper)

NAEYC item 7203

Printed on acid-free paper
Manufactured in the United States of America

14 13 12 11 10 09 08 07   8 7 6 5 4 3 2 1

Contents

Foreword

THE CONSEQUENCES OF not learning to read and write are enormous. Literacy is essential if people are to navigate school, and ultimately find jobs and participate in the social life of the broader community. In the past, children who did not learn to read and write well either dropped out of school or were diverted into vocational education. Either way, there were many social and economic opportunities available to them. This is no longer the case. As we move from an industrial to a technological society, there are new expectations for what all children will know and be able to do to meet future challenges. Today, we must teach not just some children to be literate, but all children—poor, middle-class, and rich children; black, white, and brown children; typically developing children and children with special needs and handicapping conditions.

Unfortunately, the window of opportunity for teaching is relatively brief and closes early. Statistics tell us that American children who are not on their way to learning to read and write well by third grade are at greatly increased risk of school failure. Preschool children who do not learn the precursors of reading and writing are on the track to school failure. This is why politicians, business people, community activists, educators, and citizens are interested in early literacy education and are putting it on the front burner of public concern.

Reading and writing, like speaking and drawing, are special ways of communicating. But they are not as natural. Children learn to speak and draw without a great deal of direct teaching. They learn to talk in every language in every community, despite great variations in languages and learning styles. Similarly, give children a stick, or crayons, and they will quickly draw on dirt, or on paper, or on the living room walls. There is something in the human blueprint that makes learning language and graphics natural. However, reading and writing are not the same. They must be taught.

How and when children learn to be literate varies from individual to individual and from group to group. While children from low-income families and those with special needs often have difficulty learning to read and write, many typically developing children from advantaged homes may also find literacy learning a significant challenge and need to learn using different strategies. There is considerable difference in the speed and sequence with which all children acquire literacy skills; some learn quickly and easily, some slowly and painfully.

The one constant is the need for good teaching. Fast learners, slow learners, rich children, poor children, black, white, and brown children all profit from a good literacy curriculum. And that is what Dorothy Strickland and Shannon Riley-Ayers provide in this book. They begin by pointing out that teaching for literacy should not conflict with developmentally appropriate practice, and they show how to plan so that it does not. Their book reflects the best and latest research in how to prevent reading difficulties by laying a firm foundation in preschool. This is a practitioner-friendly book and gives numerous activities that support learning. It is a useful book for students starting their careers, for experienced teachers catching up on "what's new," and for coaches and supervisors establishing an effective literacy program. It is a "must read" for anyone who wants to start children out right learning—and enjoying—literacy.

—Barbara T. Bowman

Preface

EARLY CHILDHOOD EDUCATION is receiving enormous attention in the classroom and in the public policy arena. Much of that attention is focused on early literacy and school readiness. The literacy education of young children is frequently a topic of scrutiny with resulting demands for accountability and change.

Early childhood professionals at the preschool (or prekindergarten) level, in particular, have always been aware of the importance of language and literacy. They correctly seek to plan and implement programs that are grounded in what is known about child development in the early years, reflect consistency and continuity with kindergarten and primary grade programs, employ multiple assessments that reveal useful information for program development, and link home and school in common goals. They realize that accomplishing these goals may require major changes in policies involving standards and accountability for children, programs, and the professionals responsible for them. Competent leadership is essential. Today's preschool leaders are asked to do more, know more, and produce "results."

It was with these ideas in mind that we decided to write this book. In essence, it is a quick and handy reference for today's highly challenged and very busy early childhood leaders. The book is organized so that it may be read from cover to cover or entered at key points of particular interest to the reader. Chapter 1 contains an overview of the challenges facing those responsible for preschool programs. Topics include increased expectations for children, teachers, and administrators and the complications that accompany a changing school population. Chapter 2 continues with a discussion of several key aspects of child development that are foundational for literacy. Children's physical, social, emotional, cognitive, and language development are discussed along with implications for literacy learning and teaching. Developing and using early literacy standards is the topic of Chapter 3. This is a relatively new area of concern among early childhood educators at the preschool level. It has important implications for program planning and for assessment.

Chapters 4 and 5 deal with issues related to curriculum content and effective instructional practices. This is followed by Chapter 6 on assessment and accountability, which offers a variety of practical ideas for monitoring student achievement and for linking accountability with standards and the curriculum.

The final chapters offer suggestions for providing ongoing professional development (Chapter 7), for planning effective home–school connections (Chapter 8), and for acting as advocates for children in the early childhood policy arena (Chapter 9). Attention is given, throughout the book, to issues related to the increasing linguistic and cultural diversity among children and families in preschool settings. All chapters end with one or more "Leadership Strategies" that serve as a quick guide for action and reflection on particular topics. At the end of the book are a list of pertinent resources and a glossary of terms.

Every attempt is made to link what is known about being a successful leader to what is known about the effective administration and supervision of early literacy programs. As Roskos and Vukelich (2006) aptly state:

> What early literacy policy accomplishes in the next decades depends not only on the structures placed on and in settings and programs, but also on the people who act on those structures to create patterns of activity that can either advance, resist or stall change. (p. 305)

We believe that informed leadership will play a key role in advancing early childhood education and that this book can help accomplish that goal.

Acknowledgments

WE WOULD LIKE to thank W. Steven Barnett, Director of the National Institute for Early Education Research, for the inspiration and support he provided for the policy brief that led to this book and for the book as well. Our thanks to Barbara Bowman for her excellent Foreword. We were greatly assisted by the helpful critique and advice provided by Yadira Trimino, Director of the Kids World Early Learning Center in West New York, New Jersey. We also extend our gratitude to Nancy Stirling, Supervisor of Early Childhood in Asbury Park, New Jersey, for her assistance in arranging for us to photograph the teachers and children at work in the Cares on the Square Preschool and to the teachers Jamie Clark and Alasia Connier, and to co-owners Linda Francese and Janice Ferrari, for allowing us to visit their classrooms. They help bring our words to life. We are grateful to Tim Ayers, Rebecca Brittain, and Gwynnith Strickland for their assistance with the photography. A very special thanks to the wonderful preschool class at Cares on the Square, who are depicted throughout the book.

Literacy Leadership in Early Childhood

THE ESSENTIAL GUIDE

social well-being, fewer grade retentions, and reduced incidences of juvenile delinquency, and that these outcomes are all factors associated with later adult productivity (Barnett, 2002; Bowman, Donovan, & Burns, 2000; National Institute of Child Health and Development Early Child Care Research Network, 2005; Shonkoff & Phillips, 2000; Storch & Whitehurst, 2002; Strickland & Barnett, 2003). This research pointed to early literacy as an area of particular significance, prompting still more research to identify the key early language and literacy predictors for reading and school success. As a result, much more is known today about what educators can do to promote long-term language and literacy achievement.

Ironically, many school administrators come to their positions with little background in literacy education. They soon find out that much of their time is spent working toward educational reform that centers on language and literacy. While this responsibility has traditionally been recognized as the work of K–8 administrators, the need for early childhood administrators at prekindergarten programs to know more about literacy learning and teaching is now recognized as an essential part of their background knowledge.

KEY CHALLENGES IN LITERACY EDUCATION

Today's early childhood leaders need to have a strong working knowledge of the general principles of literacy learning and teaching and what those principles look like in operation. They need to be aware of the changes in the field and how to observe instruction in an informed way to ask good questions related to materials, instruction, and assessment. Following are some of the key challenges in literacy education faced by early childhood educational leaders today.

What it means to be literate in our society has changed.

The basics have changed. While it is still true that becoming literate involves the development of some very basic skills and strategies, low-level basic skills that merely involve surface-level decoding and the recall of information are hardly enough. It is not only what we are required to do with texts that has changed; the texts themselves have changed. Texts are presented to us and generated by us in endless variety: books, magazines, and pamphlets of every conceivable design; letters and memoranda arriving via fax, e-mail, and surface mail; images on television screens, computer screens, and numerous other electronic screens and displays in our kitchens as well as our offices; and the indecipherable array of documentation for every thing we buy that must be assembled, cared for, or operated. The list goes on and on. Today's learners need literacy skills that help them adapt to constant change. The definition of what it means to be literate has evolved with the increasing demands of all aspects of our lives—personal, social, and economic. Thus, becoming and being literate is a complex endeavor, and it begins during the early childhood years.

Implications for Early Childhood Leaders. Effective early childhood leaders provide direction to schools and classrooms in which young children learn that speaking, listening, reading, and writing are important ways to communicate with one another. Children listen as someone reads to them. They discuss what is read. They may draw pictures about what is discussed and attempt to label them. They may share what they have done with others. They routinely use a variety of written texts in their classrooms—books, charts, and magazines—as well as computers and other forms of technology. They are exposed to many forms of writing, including stories, informational books, and poetry. Thus, long before they are immersed in the more formal instruction of the elementary grades, they have learned what it means to communicate successfully.

Expectations for student performance have increased.

National, state, and local school reform efforts have raised expectations for what readers and writers should know and be able to do. Public awareness of the critical need for proficient readers and writers has never been greater. Nor has public criticism of the job the schools are doing. The criticism has highlighted preschool education as an important link in the overall education of children. Today's policy makers often talk of prekindergarten through grade 12, rather than kindergarten through 12. The debate has stimulated an unprecedented amount of open dissension about the content of the preschool curriculum, much of which has focused on literacy education.

Implications for Early Childhood Leaders. Effective early childhood leaders are knowledgeable about the increased expectations for all learners in their district and state. They are familiar with the standards at all grade levels and intimate with standards at the levels for which they are responsible. They take care to go beyond what the standards say to what they mean in actual practice. What does this standard look like in the classroom? What can I do to help inspire and promote good instruction that addresses the standards in a manner that is developmentally appropriate?

Expectations for teacher performance have increased.

The need for career-long, high-quality teacher education and professional development to improve literacy instruction is highlighted in research reviews, most notably, *Preventing Reading Difficulties in Young Children* (Snow, Burns, & Griffin, 1998). In addition, many states and nongovernmental agencies have developed standards for teacher performance and/or teacher education and professional development. These are frequently linked to content standards for students. Improving the quality of teachers has emerged at the forefront of educational reform. Although distinctions are made between the beginning teacher who is just starting a career and the more seasoned professional, expectations have increased for all teachers. There is a firm realization that high-quality teacher education and continued professional development are essential to effective teaching and learning. Efforts to improve teacher quality in the areas of language arts/reading are receiving special attention.

Implications for Early Childhood Leaders. Effective early childhood leaders are aware that teacher education is an ongoing process. They plan for professional development that is connected to a long-term vision and includes all members of the staff. They provide opportunities for teachers and teacher assistants to meet on a regular basis with others who have similar responsibilities (same age groups), and they meet periodically with those who work with younger or older children. Finding the time and the staff to "cover" classrooms to encourage this kind of professional growth is a high priority. Leaders attend professional development workshops along with teachers, so that they can discuss what is heard and follow through with faculty and staff as partners.

Accountability for student achievement is at the center of school reform.

Increased demands for accountability go hand-in-hand with the move toward more universal offering of preschool education. Policy makers and the public see the need for preschool education. However, they want some assurance that they are "getting their money's worth." Accountability for improving student performance in the language arts takes many forms. At the very least, setting and implementing standards for students and teachers represent key elements of accountability. Increased emphasis on student assessment represents another attempt to be more accountable, resulting in a growing trend to include more formal measures of accountability at the preschool level. In some cases this has led to assessments more similar to those in use at elementary school levels, where standardized tests are generally the centerpiece of accountability and the barometer by which students, teachers, and school districts are measured. For better or worse, these tests have often had a profound effect on the curriculum and on some of the new trends described earlier.

Implications for Early Childhood Leaders. Effective early childhood leaders do not shy away from accountability. Rather, they think and plan in terms of putting an accountability system in place that includes regular and systematic reviews of the curriculum, ongoing professional development to maintain teacher quality, and multiple means of assessing student progress. They advocate for assessment tools that are developmentally appropriate and sensitive to the linguistic and cultural backgrounds of their students. Student assessment tools may range from observation checklists to more formal assessments mandated district-wide. Effective leaders help teachers use the assessments in an integrated manner to inform instruction and report to parents and others who share responsibility for the children they teach.

The demographics of the student population have changed.

Compounding the challenges that early childhood leaders face as they address reform is the growing diversity among the student body. This diversity reflects a changing population that is becoming increasingly rich in its multicultural and multilingual nature. The number of children in our schools whose home language is not English continues to grow rapidly and presents a challenge for teachers to learn as much as they can about successful strategies for working with them.

Implications for Early Childhood Leaders. Effective early childhood leaders foster an atmosphere throughout their school that is culturally and linguistically responsive. They take leadership in demonstrating a welcoming attitude to parents and children of all backgrounds. All teachers are urged to learn as much as they can about the home language and culture of the children they teach. Professional development activities include special attention to the needs of English learners.

LEADERSHIP STRATEGIES

To help you assess yourself and your school, we present two tools. Figure 1.1 offers a process for self-assessment of your role as an educational leader. You can review and reflect on the attributes listed in the figure. Note where you think you are doing well and where you might want to improve. Choose one or two characteristics to focus on at a time. Periodically review the list as a self-monitoring process.

FIGURE 1.1 Characteristics of an Effective Early Childhood Leader

1. Considers the development of literacy as a priority
2. Inspires faculty and children to do their best
3. Provides moral support
4. Provides support through acquisition of books and materials
5. Provides support through opportunities for professional development
6. Offers leadership through special events celebrating literacy
7. Becomes involved in literacy activities with children
8. Becomes involved in professional organizations
9. Is available to children, parents, and teachers
10. Is a good listener to children

Offers encouragement to ALL

Figure 1.2 involves taking a critical look at the literacy environment of the school as a whole. When you walk around your school building, observe and reflect on the questions in the figure. Then set aside part of a staff meeting to discuss, in general terms, your observations. Enlist the faculty's help in addressing both strengths and concerns. This could be a powerful way to get faculty to address an issue of mutual concern at school-wide and age/grade levels.

FIGURE 1.2 Assessing the School Environment

1. What would a visitor see when he or she entered the building?
   What do you think would be the first impression?
   Is there evidence that literacy learning is taking place?
2. What impression do you get of the overall climate of the school?
   From the school reception area?
   From the teachers' room?
   From the entry and departure locations where parents drop off and
      pick up their children?
3. How are the classrooms arranged?
   What is the configuration of tables? Of centers?
   Do you observe clutter? Cleanliness?
   How is children's work displayed?
   Are the physical arrangements inviting to children and conducive to
      effective learning?
4. During times especially focused on literacy instruction, what are
      the characteristics of the physical arrangements and quality of
      classroom climate? What other opportunities are present for
      literacy learning throughout the day?
5. How would you characterize the interaction between students and
      teachers?
   Between students and teacher assistants?
   Between teachers and teacher assistants?
   How would you characterize the overall learning environment?

Early Literacy and Child Development

ALTHOUGH MOST EDUCATORS and policy makers agree that a strong start in early literacy is critical, there is less agreement about how this will be accomplished. A major concern is how to maintain the established mission of early childhood care and education—which has traditionally stressed the physical, social, emotional, and overall cognitive welfare of children and their families—and strengthen the academic curriculum at the same time. Some express concern about what they perceive as a growing trend toward an overemphasis on early literacy and the creation of a curriculum imbalance. They caution against early

to the way living organisms adapt and organize the world around them. Children adapt to new information and experiences in order to maintain a sense of mental balance or equilibrium. The Piagetian view of play opened the door to consideration of the relationship between pretend play and overall cognitive and language development and the possible role of play in furthering development in these areas (Morrow & Schickedanz, 2006). Skinner relied heavily on the belief that external, environmental forces (i.e., rewards and punishments) modify our behavior. Because Vygotsky believed in the social origins of knowledge, he focused his attention on the social interaction between children and adults. He was particularly interested in the development of complex thinking. His notion of the *zone of proximal development* (ZPD) has influenced the way many teachers think about teaching. The ZPD is the level at which a child finds a task too difficult to complete alone but possible with the assistance of an adult or more experienced peer.

Implications for Early Literacy. Effective leaders are familiar with the work of major learning theorists. They function as informed observers when they visit classrooms. They know that to a greater or lesser degree, competent teachers incorporate, into the curriculum, techniques based on all the theorists described. For example, competent teachers know that children use their background knowledge, both correctly and sometimes mistakenly, to make sense of new information. When discussing a book read aloud that includes information outside of the immediate background knowledge of most of the children in a group, effective teachers anticipate cognitive challenges and mediate new learning by helping children bridge the known to the unknown and make sense of the text. They offer opportunities for children to engage in symbolic play in which objects and activities represent creations of their imaginations. The play becomes more imaginative and decontextualized as children become older and more mature, paving the way for the even greater decontextualized activities of reading and writing.

Competent teachers sometimes organize instruction into incremental steps that systematically reinforce and encourage more complex behaviors and involve elements of positive reinforcement. They provide opportunities for children to recognize their names with a graphic symbol of some sort before they are expected to recognize it with the printed letters alone. Both of these would precede expectations that children would be able to select their name when it is embedded in a list of other names. Each progressive step would be organized to provide positive reinforcement to the child.

The concept of the zone of proximal development has been particularly helpful to teachers of early literacy as they attempt to understand their role in the early phases of learning and in matching their support to learners' needs. By determining the best point of entry for teaching and learning and then providing scaffolds to move learners toward increasing independence, children gradually take more and more control of a particular aspect of their own learning.

Scaffolding is an ongoing process in which teachers continually intervene, where needed, in the learning process as children embrace challenges that reach beyond their current levels of skill and knowledge. For example, when teachers read aloud from big books, allowing children to see the text, and when they think aloud as they compose sentences on charts, they are modeling reading and writing processes. When teachers invite children to collaborate in these processes, they provide opportunities for them to think and behave as readers and writers. And, when teachers encourage children to "try out" what they know on their own, they move them toward greater and greater independence. At its earliest stages, "trying out" generally takes the form of "pretend" reading and writing. The "trying out" becomes more and more conventional, as teachers continually model literacy for children and involve them in collaborative literacy activities that provide just the right amount of challenge to move them forward in the acquisition of new knowledge and skills. The concept of the zone of proximal development is constant and evolving throughout, as teachers observe to see where students are and how to best match the scaffolding process to their needs.

Inherent in fostering children's abilities to take responsibility for their own learning is support for the development of self-regulation and self-monitoring. Effective teachers provide numerous literacy activities in which children have opportunities to evaluate and modify their efforts. They engage in self-regulation as they adjust their actions based on the potential or actual outcome of their decisions. For example, when teachers engage children in response to literature or in the creation of a written chart, the children are encouraged to recognize and recall content and demonstrate their comprehension of what was read and of what needs to be written down. They apply what they know about how texts work (i.e., stories are different from informational books; the title goes at the beginning) and analyze texts to check on where something was pictured or written or where the next word should go in something they are "helping" to write. During these processes, they continually demonstrate emerging control over their efforts as they make decisions appropriate to what they think is best and then adjust those decisions as new information unfolds. Teaching for thinking, self-regulation, and the development and extension of children's world knowledge may be the most important elements of cognition related to early language and literacy development.

Language Development

From the moment of birth, humans begin learning language, learning about language, and learning through language (Halliday, 1969). Infants and toddlers listen as adults talk and read to them. They learn that listening and talking are pleasant activities. They learn how to take turns talking and how to use language to get what they want. Before age 5 or 6, most children have mastered most of the conventions of oral language. They know the sounds in their language, its meanings and syntax or structure. They have also gained a relatively high degree of communicative competence, the knowledge and use of the social and linguistic rules that govern different situations. They are adroit and flexible in their use of language. They learn quickly that language at the dinner table is different from that used on the playground, and they have little difficulty acquiring more than one language. In learning a second language they follow a process similar to that used to acquire the first (Rueda & Garcia, 2002). For example, as with first-language learners, children learning English as a second language will develop their listening abilities much more quickly than their speaking abilities. These remarkable accomplishments provide the foundation for language and literacy learning throughout life.

Implications for Early Literacy. Language and literacy learning are inextricably interwoven. Standards for early literacy reflect this relationship. The links between language and literacy are particularly evident during interactive storybook reading where

community of educators with a shared vision of what they want their early literacy program to be. Figure 2.1 is offered as a tool to promote discussion about the personal beliefs of faculty regarding how children learn and develop literacy. This kind of activity is often used to develop a statement of philosophy for use in planning for curriculum reform.

FIGURE 2.1 Developing a Shared Vision of Literacy Education

Ask teachers to consider the following questions individually, then at grade-level meetings, and finally at whole-school meetings.

1. Who are our students?
2. What special characteristics and qualities of our students need to be addressed? How are we addressing them?
3. What assistance might be needed outside of the school (e.g., social services), and how are these being addressed?
4. What do parents expect from our school? In what ways are we attempting to find out?
5. How are we helping parents know our expectations from the home?
6. Who are we as school faculty? Are we primarily veteran teachers or relatively new teachers? Are we eager to innovate and try new things, or are we rather conservative about change?
7. Do we have a fairly consistent philosophy about literacy education and education in general?
8. Does our literacy curriculum reflect cohesive and well-articulated planning?
9. What steps can we take to develop an action plan to address any concerns we may have?

CHAPTER 3

Developing and Using Early Literacy Standards

THE GROWING TREND to generate standards for early childhood education may be the best indication of a felt need to specify curriculum content and child outcomes for early education programs. Kendall and Marzano (2004) offer at least three principal reasons for the development and use of standards: to establish clarity of curriculum content, to raise expectations for the achievement of all children, and to ensure accountability for public education. It has only been in recent years, however, that the field of early education has been a part of the standards movement. Typically, young children under the age of 5 had not been included in national content area standards, nor in local or statewide curricula. Although a latecomer, the field of early education has entered the world of standards and standard setting for programs, teacher preparation, and curriculum (Seefeldt, 2005).

It is helpful to become acquainted with the terms generally used to discuss standards. According to Shore, Bodrova, and Leong (2004), *program standards* refer to those resources, activities, and instruction that programs offer children. *Classroom standards* include such things as the maximum number of children in a classroom, teacher–pupil ratios, and the materials and supports available. *Teaching and curriculum standards* are described as the opportunities offered students to learn. *Child-outcome standards* describe the knowledge and skills that children are expected to acquire over a given period of time. Child outcome standards are sometimes accompanied by *benchmarks* that provide descriptions of the knowledge and skills children are expected to develop during a given period of time. Benchmarks are used as points of reference for progress monitoring. These terms are further explained in the glossary provided in this book.

DEVELOPMENT OF EARLY LANGUAGE AND LITERACY STANDARDS

National Organizations' Standards

Because oral language and literacy are so highly interrelated, the National Center on Education and the Economy (2001) produced a comprehensive standards document on speaking and listening for preschool through 3rd grade to accompany a previously published document that only focused on standards for reading and writing. Preschool standards for oral language are listed under the following headings:

1. *Habits*—talking a lot, talking to one's self, conversing at length on a topic, and discussing books
2. *Kinds of talk and resulting genres*—narratives, explaining and seeking information, getting things done, and producing and responding to performances

3. *Language use and conventions*—rules of interaction, wordplay, phonological awareness and language awareness, and vocabulary and word choice

Each topic is described in terms of real-life settings with implications for instruction and applications to different cultures and linguistic settings. These standards are worth noting here, since they were developed to provide the underpinning and support for literacy learning.

To illustrate, a listing of the expectations (standards) for preschool children under the heading of *Habits*, is below. This list suggests the kinds of activities in which young children should engage, with success, as they internalize and develop their dispositions toward and uses of language.

Preschool children are expected to:

- talk daily for various purposes;
- engage in play using talk to enact or extend a story line (for example, taking on roles, using different voices, solving problems);
- playfully manipulate language (including nonsense words, rhymes, silly songs, repetitious phrases);
- express ideas, feelings, and needs;
- listen and respond to direct questions;
- ask questions;
- talk and listen in small groups (during playtime or mealtime or more formally at workshop areas or craft tables); and
- share and talk daily about their own experiences, products, or writing (for example, explaining their pictures or "reading" their writing attempts). (p. 48)

Another example of a national effort to produce early language and literacy standards is the National Association for the Education of Young Children (NAEYC) Accreditation Performance Criteria for early childhood programs. Figure 3.1 presents the curriculum standards included in the NAEYC document for language development and early literacy development. These standards provide guidelines for the establishment of goals for the content that children are learning, the planned activities linked to these goals, the daily schedule and routines, and the availability and use of materials for children.

Figure 3.1 NAEYC Early Childhood Program Standards: Language Development and Early Literacy Development

The appropriate age groups for the performance criteria are designated as follows: U = universal, all ages; I = infant; T = toddler/twos; P = preschool; K = kindergarten.

	LANGUAGE DEVELOPMENT
P–K	Goals and objectives for children's acquisition of language align with the program philosophy and consider family and community perspectives.
U	Curriculum guides teachers to value and support children's oral and written communication in a language their family uses or understands.
U	Children have varied opportunities to develop competence in verbal and nonverbal communication by responding to questions; communicating needs, thoughts, and experiences; and describing things and events.
T–P–K	Curriculum guides teachers to support alternative communication strategies for children who are nonverbal.
U	Children have varied opportunities to develop vocabulary through conversations, experiences, field trips, and books.
P–K	Children have varied opportunities and materials that encourage them to have discussions to solve problems that are both interpersonal and related to the physical world.
P–K	Children have varied opportunities and are provided materials that encourage them to engage in discussions with one another.
	EARLY LITERACY DEVELOPMENT
P–K	Children have varied opportunities to • be read books in an engaging manner at least twice daily in full-day programs and at least once daily in half-day programs in group or individualized settings. • be read to in individualized ways including one to one or in small groups of two to six children regularly. • explore books on their own and have places that are conducive to the quiet enjoyment of books. • have access to various types of books including storybooks, factual books, books with rhymes, alphabet books, and wordless books. • be read the same book on repeated occasions. • retell or reenact events in storybooks.

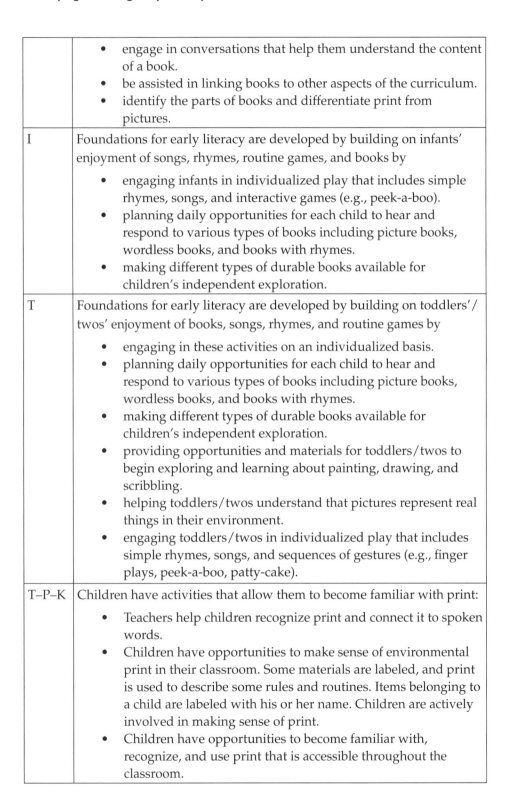

	<ul><li>engage in conversations that help them understand the content of a book.</li><li>be assisted in linking books to other aspects of the curriculum.</li><li>identify the parts of books and differentiate print from pictures.</li></ul>
I	Foundations for early literacy are developed by building on infants' enjoyment of songs, rhymes, routine games, and books by <ul><li>engaging infants in individualized play that includes simple rhymes, songs, and interactive games (e.g., peek-a-boo).</li><li>planning daily opportunities for each child to hear and respond to various types of books including picture books, wordless books, and books with rhymes.</li><li>making different types of durable books available for children's independent exploration.</li></ul>
T	Foundations for early literacy are developed by building on toddlers'/twos' enjoyment of books, songs, rhymes, and routine games by <ul><li>engaging in these activities on an individualized basis.</li><li>planning daily opportunities for each child to hear and respond to various types of books including picture books, wordless books, and books with rhymes.</li><li>making different types of durable books available for children's independent exploration.</li><li>providing opportunities and materials for toddlers/twos to begin exploring and learning about painting, drawing, and scribbling.</li><li>helping toddlers/twos understand that pictures represent real things in their environment.</li><li>engaging toddlers/twos in individualized play that includes simple rhymes, songs, and sequences of gestures (e.g., finger plays, peek-a-boo, patty-cake).</li></ul>
T–P–K	Children have activities that allow them to become familiar with print: <ul><li>Teachers help children recognize print and connect it to spoken words.</li><li>Children have opportunities to make sense of environmental print in their classroom. Some materials are labeled, and print is used to describe some rules and routines. Items belonging to a child are labeled with his or her name. Children are actively involved in making sense of print.</li><li>Children have opportunities to become familiar with, recognize, and use print that is accessible throughout the classroom.</li></ul>

K	Children have varied opportunities to learn to read familiar words, sentences, and simple books.
P–K	Children have multiple and varied opportunities to write: • Writing is embedded into art, dramatic play, and various center activities, and writing materials are readily available for use in these areas. • Children have daily opportunities to write or dictate their ideas. • Various types of writing are supported, including scribbling, letter-like marks, and developmental spelling. • Children are given the support they need to write on their own, including access to the alphabet (e.g., displayed at eye level or on laminated cards) and printed words about topics of current interest. • Children are provided needed assistance in writing the words and messages they are trying to communicate. • Children see teachers model functional use of writing and are helped to discuss the many ways writing is used in daily life.
K	Each child is encouraged to write independently each day.
P–K	Children are regularly provided multiple and varied opportunities to develop phonological awareness: • They are encouraged to play with the sounds of language, including syllables, word families, and phonemes using rhymes, poems, songs, and finger plays. • They are helped to identify letters and the sounds they represent. • They are helped to recognize and produce words that have the same beginning or ending sounds. • They are supported in their self-initiated efforts to write letters that represent the sounds of words.
P–K	Children are given opportunities to recognize and write letters.
K	Children are encouraged to identify phonemes in words through varied activities, including writing and games.
P–K	Books are displayed and writing is encouraged in one or more areas of the classroom.

Note: Language Development and Early Literacy Development Criteria, excerpted from Program Standard 2—Curriculum, of the 2005 National Association for the Education of Young Children Early Childhood Program Standards and Accreditation Criteria. In *NAEYC Early Childhood Program Standards and Accreditation Criteria: The Mark of Quality in Early Childhood Education* (Washington, DC: NAEYC, 2005), 20–2. Reprinted with permission.

A helpful document for administrators and teachers who work with children learning English as a second language is *ESL Standards for Pre-K–12 Students* (Teachers of English to Speakers of Other Languages, 1997). Documents of this type are useful for developing local curriculum and for articulating the prekindergarten curriculum with later grade levels. The standards include three broad goals for English Language Learners regardless of grade level. Each goal is accompanied by more specific standards, each with accompanying vignettes and discussion.

- *Goal 1.* To use English to communicate in social settings
- *Goal 2.* To use English to achieve academically in all content areas
- *Goal 3.* To use English in socially and culturally appropriate ways

State Standards

In addition to national efforts, such as those described above, individual states have embraced the standards movement. In 2005, 43 states reported early childhood standards, which is a substantial increase over the past few years (Neuman & Roskos, 2005). Examination of these showed that the state content standards include language and literacy. Specifically, the standards represent oral language development, phonological awareness, print knowledge and use, and writing.

Our review revealed considerable variability in presentation, terminology, and substance across the states. Numerous states have developed *content standards* (Hawaii, Illinois, Alabama), whereas other documents present *early learning guidelines* (Nebraska), *expectations* (New Jersey), and *curricular goals and benchmarks* (Connecticut). States also differ in the support or substance provided in the document. In particular, many states provide supportive information for the standards presented in the form of student examples and performance indicators (Georgia, Virginia, Florida), and some provide instructional suggestions for teachers. For example, New Jersey offers preschool teaching practices for each standard, Massachusetts provides ideas for learning experiences with each learning guideline, and Minnesota provides strategies for community members, policy makers, and family members for each of their early childhood indicators of progress. The District of Columbia presents content standards followed by a chart containing performance standards, essential skills, and additional technology integration. In the standards reviewed, this was the only document that created a prominent and direct connection to technology language and literacy. A few states, such as Arizona and Colorado, attended to continuity across grade levels by explicitly referencing K–12 standards for each prekindergarten standard offered. Figure 3.2 offers examples of standards found in several state documents.

EXPECTATIONS FOR TEACHERS

By their very nature, the standards that focus on child outcomes or curriculum content also imply what is expected of teachers. Nevertheless, there are specific efforts by national organizations that attempt to outline what early childhood teachers of English language arts should know and be able to do (see the International Reading Association [IRA], 2003; IRA & National Association for the Education of Young Children, 1998; and the National Board for Professional Teaching Standards, 2001). These documents address foundational knowledge related to the following:

- Reading and writing processes
- Language development and reading acquisition and the variations related to cultural and linguistic diversity
- The major components of early reading (phonological awareness, vocabulary development, background knowledge, and so forth)
- The use of appropriate practices to promote language and literacy development

Today's educators generally agree that the quality of a teacher affects children's achievement. Increased attention to the need for high-quality preparation and ongoing support of early childhood literacy teachers has resulted. Vukelich (2004) suggests that much more needs to be done to define the specific pedagogical skills necessary to be an effective early childhood literacy teacher. Nevertheless, early childhood leaders have a responsibility to help move staff forward in improving knowledge and skills. Use of existing teacher standards can provide helpful guidance. In Chapter 7 we offer some examples of teacher standards taken from a range of teacher competencies in early literacy developed by a state department of education.

FIGURE 3.2 Examples of State Standards for Early Language and Literacy (Prekindergarten)

KEY ASPECT	STATE STANDARDS
Oral Language • Listening comprehension • Verbal expression • Vocabulary development	**New York:** During prekindergarten, students are developing listening competencies in order to listen attentively to spoken language (e.g., books read aloud, rhyming words, songs), listen attentively for different purposes (e.g., to track individual words as they are spoken, to gain information), understand and follow oral directions, and listen respectfully without interrupting others. **New Jersey:** Children converse effectively in their home language, English, or sign language for a variety of purposes relating to real experiences and different audiences.
Alphabetic Code • Knowledge of alphabet letters • Phonological awareness	**Colorado:** Preschool learners begin to become phonemically aware—the ability to hear separate sounds. They are learning that speech is composed of individual sounds, that words are composed of syllables and sounds, that some words rhyme, and that sounds can be manipulated.
Print Knowledge and Use • Environmental print • Concepts about print	**Missouri:** Applies early reading skills: shows interest in reading and books, exhibits book-handling skills, pretends to read easy or predictable books or tries to read along during his or her favorite part of the story, responds to text, reads environmental print and symbols, identifies some alphabet letters, recognizes that print represents spoken words, and develops a sense of story.
Writing	**Louisiana:** Engage in activities that promote the acquisition of emergent writing skills: experiment with a variety of writing tools, materials, and surfaces; use early stages of writing in the form of shapes and letter-like symbols to convey ideas; participate in a variety of writing activities focused on meaningful words and print in the environment; and demonstrate an interest in using writing for a purpose.

Sources: Colorado State Department of Education (2003); Louisiana State Department of Education (2003); Missouri Department of Elementary and Secondary Education Early Childhood Section (n.d.); New Jersey State Department of Education (2004); New York State Education Department & The University of the State of New York (n.d.).

LEADERSHIP STRATEGY

Attention to standards will remain a key consideration when early literacy programs are in the process of development. For that reason it is important to develop them wisely and with caution. In a joint policy statement on early learning standards the National Association for the Education of Young Children and the National Association of Early Childhood Specialists in State Departments of Education (NAECS/SDE) describe the risks and benefits of early learning standards (NAEYC & NAECS/SDE, 2002). They caution that a major risk of any standards movement is that the responsibility for meeting the standards will be placed on children's shoulders rather than on the shoulders of those who should provide opportunities and supports for learning, and suggest that culturally and linguistically diverse children, and children with disabilities, may be at heightened risk. Nevertheless, they conclude that clear, research-based expectations for the content and desired results of early learning experiences can help focus curriculum and instruction and increase the likelihood of later positive outcomes.

Figure 3.3 is offered as a guide for early childhood leaders and their staffs to reflect on their knowledge of local, state, and national standards that apply to their situation and to plan appropriate action for program improvement.

FIGURE 3.3 Self-Check on Early Literacy Standards

Use the self-inventory below to examine how informed you and your staff are about the standards in place in your district and state.

1. How familiar am I with the standards for English language arts and literacy in my district? In my state? Consider standards for programs, teachers, and children.
2. What opportunities have the faculty/staff had to review, discuss, and take action on the standards overall? Consider standards for programs, teachers, and children.
3. How have parents been informed about standards and their impact on school and home activities?
4. How well do state and district standards map to our curriculum? How are those connections reflected in the classroom?
5. How well do our current assessment practices and measures link to district and state standards?

CHAPTER 4

The Early Literacy Curriculum: Focus on Content

IN THE AREA OF literacy, both federal and state expectations have emphasized evidence-based practice to guide curriculum adoption and the evaluation of curriculum effectiveness. Evidence must be grounded in *scientifically based research,* a term used across a variety of fields, including medicine and education, to signal a set of key research characteristics. These include the application of systematic and objective procedures to obtain information about important questions in a particular field in an attempt to ensure that those who use the research can have a high degree of confidence that it is valid and dependable.

Obviously these are very high standards. Some suggest that only certain types of research meet these qualifications. Others argue that if we narrowly limit the types of research on which we rely, we may overlook important and credible studies that can inform the field. They suggest that high-quality research of various types will be needed to investigate the wide range of important questions we face. Furthermore, regardless of the type of research we turn to, it is clear that responsible local judgment will and should always play a role in its use.

Whether a curriculum is home-grown or commercially prepared, those who develop and use it are expected to support their claims with a research base. Thus all educators, including those who work with very young children, are expected to be acquainted with the research that guides their practice. Scientifically based research reminds us to thoughtfully reflect on our past assumptions, be prepared to support what we do by citing more than our own experience, and not be afraid to require the same of others (Strickland, 2004).

KEY COMPONENTS OF
THE EARLY LITERACY CURRICULUM:
EXPECTATIONS AND OPPORTUNITIES TO LEARN

An early literacy curriculum grounded in evidence-based research is comprised of the following key components:

1. Oral language development, which includes vocabulary and listening
2. An understanding of the alphabetic code, which includes phonological/phonemic awareness and knowledge of the alphabet
3. Knowledge and understanding about print and its use (Strickland & Shanahan, 2004)

Each component will be discussed separately, and figures will present these aspects of the early literacy curriculum in terms of expectations (standards) and typical opportunities to learn.

Oral Language

Developing concurrently with literacy, oral language includes listening comprehension, verbal expression, and vocabulary development. Oral language development is facilitated when children have many opportunities to use language in interactions with adults and with each other, both one-on-one and in small groups; when they are frequently engaged in extended conversations with adults; and when they listen and respond to stories read and told. Young children build vocabulary when they engage in activities that are cognitively and linguistically stimulating. These activities allow them to describe events, build background knowledge, and extend the vocabulary they have, as they build an even broader word and conceptual knowledge base. All of this must be done with special attention to the needs of English Language Learners and to those whose development may be different from the typical child. Figure 4.1 presents a list of expectations and opportunities for learning generally included in early childhood curriculum standards for oral language development.

Alphabetic Code

English is an alphabetic language, which means that the letters we use to write represent the sounds of the language that we speak. *Knowledge of the alphabet letters* and *phonological awareness* (the ability to hear the sounds within words) form the basis of early decoding and spelling ability, and both are closely correlated with later reading and spelling achievement. Young children develop a concept of letter(s) as they learn to name them, distinguish them from one another and from numbers, and understand that letters form words. They can also begin to develop an awareness of the constituent sounds within words, such as syllables, rhymes, and phonemes. Children who can hear the sounds in oral language are more likely to benefit from early reading instruction.

Phonemic awareness is the ability to hear, identify, and manipulate the individual sounds (*phonemes*) in spoken words. It is one level of phonological awareness. Activities that boost phonemic awareness build on the broad aspects of phonological awareness such as identifying and making oral rhymes and clapping or tapping syllables in spoken words. Phonemic awareness requires more specific

FIGURE 4.1 Expectations and Opportunities for Developing Oral Language (including vocabulary and listening)

Children should be able to	*Adults should provide opportunities for children to*
• Listen and identify sounds in the environment such as human speech, animal sounds, music, etc. • Listen attentively to meaningful dialogue, and to engage in discussion with others • Listen attentively and respond to books and other print materials read aloud • Carry on complete and meaningful conversations with peers and adults in increasingly complex ways • Extend and expand conversations during group discussions • Use new vocabulary introduced through firsthand or book reading experiences • Link new and known vocabulary and concepts	• Create sounds by singing; participate in music-making • Listen and respond to music and to others during discussion • Engage in shared-book experiences that require both listening and oral response • Listen for various purposes: for enjoyment, to follow directions, to engage in dialogue with others, to attend to patterns in the language • Engage cognitively and verbally in oral language activities that are linguistically stimulating and focus their attention on patterns and similarities in language • Engage in cognitively and verbally stimulating activities, based on topics of interest and expanded vocabulary

Source: Strickland & Shanahan, 2004.

skills than other levels of phonological awareness, and these skills link more directly to *phonics*, which relates sounds to the letters that represent them. Instruction in phonemic awareness may, at times, involve the use of print. That is, it may include linking the representation of a letter or letters to sounds as they are stressed or isolated in spoken words by an adult.

Children demonstrate their knowledge of the beginning levels of phonological awareness when they

- Identify and make oral rhymes.
  I can bake a chocolate (cake).
  The cat wore a (hat).
- Identify and work with syllables in spoken words.
  Children clap the syllables in spoken words.

Children demonstrate their understandings of finer aspects of phonological awareness (phonemic awareness) when they

- Identify and work with *onsets* and *rimes* in one-syllable words.
  The first part of dog is /d/
  The last part of cat is –at
- Recognize when several words begin with the same sound.
  Silly Sally saw a snake.
  Wee Willie went walking.
  Peter Piper picked a peck of pickled peppers.
- Identify words that begin with a specific sound.
  Match and sort pictures by first sound.

Phonemic awareness activities are most effective when children are taught to manipulate phonemes and to anchor or code these with letters. Thus, the activities presented above could make use of print along with the specific sounds targeted. In other words, when children learn to identify letters side-by-side with their developing awareness of the sounds in the language, it acts as a logical bridge to phonics. When 4-year-old Bobby is able to determine that the sound he hears at the beginning of his name is the same as the sound he hears at the beginning of the words *bear* and *bottle* (phonemic awareness), it will not take long for him to make the connection between that sound and the letter *Bb* (letter recognition, which he is also learning), which he sees at the beginning of words that start like his name. This is sometimes referred to as "phonological awareness with a phonics connection" (National Head Start Summer Teacher Education Program, 2002, p. 71; see also Armbruster, Lehr, & Osborn, 2001).

Children should be immersed in language-rich environments in order to develop phonological awareness, and similarly, it would be difficult to master the ABCs without lots of exposure to the alphabet (in books, on blocks, on refrigerator magnets, in cereal, in soup, and so forth). Knowledge of the ABCs and phonological awareness do not usually just happen from exposure for most children, however. Parents, teachers, and older siblings often intentionally teach children the alphabet, and studies have shown that it is possible to teach phonological awareness to preschoolers and kindergarten children in ways that improve later literacy (National Reading Panel, 2000).

A word about writing in preschool—our discussion of the alphabetic code includes information related to children's early attempts at independent writing. The use of invented or phonics-based spelling is an indication that children are beginning to make generalizations about how the language works and to apply that knowledge in order to compose. It is important to note, however, that the composing process begins well before this. Given easy access to materials with which to draw and scribble, most children will gradually begin to bridge their oral and written worlds through drawing, scribbling, making lines, mock letters, actual letters, and various combinations of these in purposeful ways. As with reading, they will observe, participate collaboratively with responsive adults, and "try out" the composing process on their own. Schickedanz and Casbergue (2004) give vivid descriptions of the adult's role in supporting children's writing. Parents and teachers respond to children's questions, sometimes make suggestions, pose questions, play with children in ways that allow them to demonstrate writing in purposeful ways (such as taking a telephone message during creative play), encourage and assist children in writing their names on their work to indicate ownership, listen while children relate what they have written, and generally celebrate their attempts to compose. Since children frequently talk at length about what they have composed, written composition may represent the ultimate blend of language and literacy development. When children write they bring together their understandings about oral and written communication, the alphabetic code, and concepts about print. Their writing also builds upon and reflects their vocabulary and conceptual development and their knowledge of the world. Figure 4.2 presents a list of expectations and opportunities for learning included in early childhood curriculum standards for mastering the alphabetic code.

Print Knowledge and Use

Making sense of print involves an awareness and understanding of environmental print and of concepts of print, such as where to begin to read a book or a page, in which direction to read, and that words have discrete boundaries (or spaces) around them. Each of these is likely learned from interacting with others around print. An early literacy curriculum might include grocery store visits; being

FIGURE 4.2 Expectations and Opportunities for Learning About the Alphabetic Code (including alphabet knowledge, phonological/phonemic awareness, and invented spelling)

ALPHABET KNOWLEDGE	
Children should be able to	*Adults should provide opportunities to*
• Recognize that alphabet letters can be named • Learn the names of 10 (note: this is now considered a minimum, even for most children with significant problems) or more letters, including those in their name	• Play with letters, alphabet puzzles • Engage with alphabet books • Participate in experiences where letter names are linked to writing, particularly their own names and others
PHONOLOGICAL/PHONEMIC AWARENESS WITH GRADUAL LINKS TO PRINT AND WRITING	
Children should be able to	*Adults should provide opportunities to*
• Identify and make oral rhymes • Identify and work with syllables in spoken words • Recognize and produce words starting with the same sound • Separate the first sound from a word (/c/ — /at/) orally • Have a general understanding that letters represent the sounds that make up spoken words (alphabetic principle) • Have a growing understanding that they can use the alphabetic code to communicate through writing	• Work with rhymes • Engage in language play • Observe others as they produce words starting with the same sound and participate in similar activities • Observe others as they segment spoken words into their individual sounds and participate in similar activities • Select letters to represent individual sounds (usually at the beginning of a word) that they have segmented in a spoken word • Participate in opportunities to write their own name • Apply what they know about the alphabetic code to write independently

Source: Strickland & Shanahan, 2004.

read to on a daily basis; having a writing center where children can experiment with written communication and environmental print that is purposeful, such as functional signs, labels, and charts. In addition, effective early literacy teachers model the reading and writing processes during shared reading and writing. They explicitly comment aloud about what they are thinking as they read and write so as to make the process transparent to children. They point out particular words in books and on charts. They track print from left to right with their hand, discuss authors and illustrators and what they do, and use the language of literacy such as title, page, word, sentence, and so on. Figure 4.3 presents a list of expectations and opportunities for learning included in early childhood curriculum standards for developing a knowledge of concepts about print.

FIGURE 4.3 Expectations and Opportunities for Developing a Knowledge of Print and Its Use (including environmental print and concepts about print)

Children should be able to	*Adults should provide opportunities for children to*
• Understand that print is used for various purposes • Understand that speech can be written down; letters make up words • Understand that print carries a message • Understand that illustrations carry meaning but cannot be read • Understand that books have titles and authors • Understand concept of a "word"—letters are grouped to form words and words are separated by spaces • Understand concept of directionality—front to back, left to right, top to bottom • Develop vocabulary to talk about print (word, letter, list, page, etc.)	• Observe adults writing as they say words aloud • Participate in the composing process by contributing ideas/language for others to write down • Participate in discussions about and use of labels, signs, and other print in the environment • Observe and follow along as adults track print from left to right while reading aloud • Independently browse through books front to back • Engage in opportunities to draw and "write" independently

Source: Strickland & Shanahan, 2004.

LEADERSHIP STRATEGIES

To provide literacy leaders with the background knowledge needed to help them become better informed observers of teachers and children during interactive literacy activities, we present two frameworks in chart form. Each framework is intended to help the observer understand what they should see and why it is important.

Engaging children in the shared (sometimes referred to as interactive) reading of big books (books with enlarged text) offers special opportunities for learning about print. Unlike most other read-aloud experiences, big books allow children to continuously see the print and pictures as a teacher reads aloud. Subsequent readings of the same book allow the teacher to point out specific aspects of the print and help children conceptualize what people do when they read. Figure 4.4 can be used as a framework for observing shared reading.

Like shared reading, shared writing offers children an opportunity to actively collaborate in a literacy activity. They go beyond the role of listener and observer to offer suggestions about what might be written down. Depending on their previous experiences with print, they might offer suggestions about spelling and spacing. Skillful teachers know the capabilities of the children they teach and prompt accordingly. Since shared writing can be time-consuming, it is suggested that teachers do it often, but for limited amounts of time. Figure 4.5 can be used as a framework for observing shared writing.

After the Writing		
• Reads completed text for children. • Rereads the text, encouraging children to join in. • Guides analysis of text by discussing ideas and noticing print patterns, such as repeated words, phrases, and letters they know. • Encourages children to try out writing on their own and provides materials and guidance at their request.	• Observes as the teacher reads the completed text. • Shares in rereading of the text to the extent possible. • Participates in analysis of text by noticing (matching) words and phrases and identifying known letters. • Attempts, independently, to communicate ideas through written expression.	• Understanding that what we write can be read by us and by others; that we can return to it again and again to reread and discuss. • Providing encouragement to children to make attempts at writing (and drawing) about things of interest and importance to them.

CHAPTER 5

The Early Literacy Curriculum: Focus on Best Practices

IN CHAPTER 4, we focused on what early childhood leaders need to know about the content of the language and literacy curriculum. In this chapter, we turn to *best practices*, the instructional strategies that foster children's learning of that content.

KEY ISSUES RELATED TO BEST PRACTICES

A literacy leader's familiarity with several key issues related to best practices can make the difference between an effective curriculum and one that flounders. These issues include

- Keeping play at the forefront of literacy learning
- Providing a print-rich environment
- Encouraging linguistically and culturally responsive teaching
- Attending to prevention and intervention
- Organizing for differentiated instruction
- Balancing skills and strategies
- Scaffolding children's learning
- Using technology wisely
- Integrating literature and literacy across the curriculum

We provide a brief description of each issue with some implications and suggestions for practice.

Keeping Play at the Forefront of Literacy Learning

A predisposition to play is inherent in children. Many of the researchers we cited in Chapter 2, especially Piaget and Vygotsky, explicitly link symbolic play with language and literacy. Early childhood educators have long been encouraged to use playful activities as a means to stimulate learning. Many teachers express concern that a focus on early literacy will gradually eliminate play from the curriculum. They worry that literacy-enriched activities will make preschool look more like kindergarten and that kindergarten will look more like 1st grade. Their fears are well founded when educators think of early literacy content as a composite body of knowledge that children must learn and spout back on demand, rather than as a symbolic system that they can acquire over time to help them make sense of their world. Indeed, there is no reason to believe that kindergarten and 1st grade literacy learning need be devoid of playful activities that encourage children's imagination, participation, and joy in learning any more than prekindergarten programs.

Implications for Practice. The best teaching strategies capitalize on children's natural propensity to explore and learn through play. This is accomplished through both teacher-led learning opportunities and through opportunities for children to apply what they know in "free" play situations. Including books, paper, and writing implements in the dramatic play area to encourage children to incorporate literacy in their play activities is just one example of providing opportunities for children to learn literacy through play.

Providing a Print-Rich Environment

One important way that young children construct knowledge and understandings about print is through experiences with logos, labels, road signs, and other meaningful visual displays found in the immediate environment. Children observe as adults use environmental print in functional ways: to make selections from a fast food menu, to stop at a stop sign, and to choose items at the supermarket. At school they may be engaged in similar ways as they find their names on a chart or as they return materials, such as crayons or scissors, to a particular labeled bin.

Implications for Practice. Effective teachers plan the environment so that children are engaged in purposeful uses of visual symbols. In print-rich classrooms opportunities for using environmental print present themselves naturally throughout the day. A checklist for examining the quality of print exposure and use in classrooms is provided at the end of this chapter in Figure 5.3. It is important to note that the display of print for its own sake without links to the curriculum or signs of active use by children is not considered to be effective. Some might even construe it to be like bland wallpaper, given little or no attention by the occupants of the room.

Encouraging Linguistically and Culturally Responsive Teaching

Issues related to a child's linguistic and cultural background represent a growing challenge for early literacy educators. In the changing demographics of our nation, preschool educators increasingly encounter children and families from a variety of cultures. Latinos, for example, are now the largest minority group in the country and are growing at a faster rate than the population as a whole (U.S. Census Bureau, 2003). Even for many English-speaking children, the school language (or dialect) and culture may differ greatly from that of their homes. Teachers of young children need to keep in mind that a child's prekindergarten classroom may be the first setting of sustained contact with a new culture and will help set the stage for early success or failure with formal schooling (Suarez-Orozco, 2001).

Implications for Practice. Early childhood professionals in effective programs seek to learn as much as they can about the cultural and linguistic backgrounds of the children with whom they work. Such teachers understand the nature of linguistic diversity and provide developmentally appropriate experiences with English language literacy for children. Family literacy programs are offered to reinforce these experiences and provide continuity between home and school. Whenever practical, such programs employ staff who speak the children's home language as well as English. In general the curriculum is implemented in ways that foster respect for what children bring to the learning situation and that provide continuity between the child's experiences at home and those within the early childhood program.

Attending to Prevention and Intervention

Studies of the relationship between early literacy development and school achievement have had a profound impact on the early literacy curriculum as an intervention process for children considered to be at risk for failure. Risk factors include

- Exhibiting a developmental disability (e.g., oral language impairment, mental retardation, hearing impairment)
- Having a parent with a history of reading disability
- Speaking a language or dialect that differs from the local academic curriculum
- Living in a household in which experiences with oral and written language are infrequent (Snow, Burns, & Griffin, 1998)

For children in such circumstances, a preventive approach to early literacy may be required to encourage timely attainment of the skills and abilities needed for later school readiness and achievement.

The curriculum components outlined in Chapter 4 are viewed as essential elements of instruction for all children. Nevertheless, children vary in how well any "basic" curriculum will serve them. They differ in what they bring to the preschool setting and what they gain from it. Some children enter preschool having had the advantage of an abundance of experiences with books and print. Their backgrounds include numerous opportunities for visits to interesting places where adults and older siblings hold conversations with them about what they observe. Equally important, they enjoy opportunities for play at home that serve to expand their general knowledge and intellectual development. For these children, both their linguistic and experiential backgrounds match well with what most schools expect. The preschool curriculum provides an opportunity to reinforce and expand the rich reservoir of skills and knowledge these children possess.

For a variety of reasons, many other children need more, different, or specifically targeted learning opportunities in preschool. Indeed, variability among any group of preschool children can be assured. Children vary in the amount and type of language and literacy experiences provided at home. They vary in their cultural and linguistic backgrounds. Some may have specific learning difficulties. Still others may simply take longer to learn than most. Moreover, several of these factors may be represented in any individual child. Justice and Pullen (2003) suggest three approaches that have strong evidence as promising preschool interventions:

1. Adult–child shared storybook reading
2. Literacy-enriched play settings
3. Teacher-directed structured phonological awareness curricula

Implications for Practice. Keep in mind that no matter how theoretically sound and well-crafted the written curriculum may be, it is only as effective as its ability to serve the differing needs of individual children. Skillful teachers are constantly alert to variability in student progress and response to instruction. They make adjustments within the framework of the curriculum in order to make instruction more responsive to student needs. When necessary they seek the advice of specialists in particular areas and resources outside of the classroom in order to adjust the curriculum even further.

Organizing for Differentiated Instruction

Differentiating instruction to meet the individual needs of learners is arguably one of the most important things that effective teachers do. Differentiation can take many forms. Varying teacher–pupil ratio is the most common way that teachers differentiate. They sometimes work with the whole group, with small groups, and with children one-to-one. Changes in teacher–pupil ratio result in important changes in the constituency of the group.

Implications for Practice. Whole-group instruction involves the entire class. It generally takes place with all of the children seated on a rug during "circle time," so called because children are often seated in a circle for instruction. By its very nature it includes the widest range of abilities and interests in the group. It is excellent for introducing and supporting specific concepts, skills, and strategies. Used diagnostically, it can help determine the need for small-group and individual follow-up. It also has the advantage of building a sense of community among the children.

Small-group instruction (generally 2–5 children) is often scheduled during "center time," a block of time in which some children work independently at various activity centers in the room while their teachers work with small groups and individuals. This type of organization allows for a more homogeneous grouping of children who have similar needs, interests, and abilities. Both small-group and one-to-one instruction are a natural follow-up to whole-group instruction. Teachers may briefly revisit specific aspects of a whole-group activity with two or three children: "Did you notice any letters that looked the same on the chart we worked on earlier?" Intervention for English Language Learners, educationally advanced children, and those with other special needs is best done with small groups.

One-to-one instruction may occur as part of center time activities or as brief, highly focused adult–child interactions throughout the day. Typical purposes and types of interaction are the same as that of small-group instruction, only individualized.

Providing for both explicit (direct) and more informal but well-planned indirect instruction is another consideration for differentiation. Explicit teaching may take place during whole-group or small-group time. Well-planned opportunities for independent work during center time allow children to work in informal ways, often applying the knowledge more explicitly.

Another way to differentiate instruction is to provide a variety of materials and modalities for children to explore and apply what they know. For example, children can improve their letter recognition through explorations with felt or wooden letters and computer software programs, and by attempts at writing letters on their own.

Literacy leaders should insist that teachers plan for differentiated instruction. Moreover, the planning should be treated as an intentional, thoughtful activity that builds on stated curriculum goals with strong links to standards and assessment.

Balancing Skills and Strategies

Effective educators throughout the grades emphasize strategy instruction over the accumulation of isolated skills. While both skills and strategies are important to early literacy instruction, early childhood leaders and teachers need to understand the difference between the two. Paris, Wasik, and Turner (1991) suggest that strategies are distinct from skills. People perform skills the same way every time. For example, recognizing the names of letters and reading from left to right are skills. Skill instruction is often accomplished through drill and repetition. Strategies are plans for solving problems encountered in constructing meaning (Duffy, 1993). Unlike skills, these plans are not automatic. Learners modify their plans—their strategies—depending on the situation. For example, how you pronounce *wind* will depend on the meaning of the sentence in which you find it: "The *wind* blew the tree down," or "Mother asked me to *wind* the clock." The reader uses the meaning of the sentence in a strategic way to decide how *wind* will be pronounced.

Implications for Practice. Understanding the distinction between a skill and a strategy is especially important when teaching phonemic awareness and letter knowledge. While it is important for children to hear the sounds in words and to name letters, this is only a small part of what they need to know. The fact that a young child can recite the alphabet is quite an accomplishment, but it is not a strategy. It is a skill. Having that skill does not mean that the child understands that letters are used to form words and that changing the order of the letters actually changes the word.

Both phonological awareness and letter knowledge may function as isolated skills that are not very helpful unless children understand how to apply them as they read and write. At that point, these skills become useful strategies. This is why we stress that teachers continually model the uses of reading and writing and actually demonstrate the process for children in a variety of formal and informal ways. As children observe how our system of language works, they begin to connect their knowledge of sounds and letters to what it means for reading and writing. They begin to ask questions about letters and words. Ultimately they begin to "try out" what they know through their own attempts to read and write.

Scaffolding Children's Learning

Scaffolding refers to the process whereby a child's learning occurs in the context of full performance as adults gradually relinquish support (Cazden, 1988). Think of the phrase "everybody needs a helping hand," and it will be easy to remember what scaffolding is. Adults frequently help children accomplish things they want to do, such as work with a puzzle, write the first letter of their name, or ride a bike. First we show them how we do it. In fact, for some time they may have been observing us doing an activity when we were in control. Now we invite them to try, and we help as they attempt to do it. At times we intervene, but only when our assistance is needed. When we think they are ready, we let them try completely on their own (Strickland & Schickedanz, 2004).

Implications for Practice. When a teacher reads aloud or models writing for children, he or she has full control of the process. The children watch and learn what skilled readers and writers do. When a teacher invites children to join in as he or she reads from familiar big books or engages children in writing a chart, they are involved in the process. The children participate as much as they can. Their understanding deepens as the teacher guides them to read a repeated phrase in a book or prompts them to suggest a word to be written on a chart. Throughout, children are systematically involved in observing and participating in literacy activities, leading to opportunities to "try out" reading and writing on their own. Effective teachers use scaffolding to plan and guide instruction that moves from teacher control to child independence. Literacy leaders should be watchful for this type of instruction in the classrooms they observe.

Using Technology Wisely

Virtually all of today's young children are immersed in a world of technology. This is true regardless of their cultural or economic backgrounds. They come to preschool already familiar with television, VCRs, CD players, computers, cell phones, and iPods. Nevertheless, many educators remain cautious about the use of technology in the classroom. Teachers are concerned that time spent at computers may be at the expense of more valuable time spent involving hands-on opportunities for learning and exploring the environment. They worry that the use of television programs designed especially for language and literacy development may appear to others as an excuse or substitute for providing their own instruction. Yet the selective and limited use of language and literacy programs may be appropriate for the classroom, especially when they are accompanied by teacher-support materials.

Implications for Practice. Some teachers are unfamiliar with what is available in the way of technological support and have little experience or training in its use. Others lack the background knowledge required to incorporate technology into the existing curriculum. In such cases teachers may have access to computers and other types of technology, but they are either used poorly or not at all. For example, simply allowing children to aimlessly operate software programs with no preparation or support is a waste of time. As with any kind of independent activity, teachers should model the use of a new software program for the entire group before children are allowed to use it on their own. Follow-up monitoring of children's use is also important.

It seems prudent for literacy leaders to become better informed about the possible uses of technology. Taking advantage of technical support from the school district or appropriately trained university educators who specialize in this area would make an excellent year-long professional development project for the entire staff. Topics explored could include shoring up the knowledge and skills of classroom teachers and other personnel in the use of technology, learning how to evaluate and select computer software, and planning for the inclusion of technology as one of many tools that support literacy learning. Later in this chapter, Figure 5.4 offers a checklist to use when evaluating computer software for purchase.

Integrating Literature and Literacy Across the Curriculum

The need to help teachers pull all the pieces of the curriculum into an integrated whole is among the greatest challenges facing literacy leaders. None of the elements described in this chapter should stand alone. All assume that the language and literacy program is equipped with an adequate supply of excellent children's literature and that there are ample opportunities for children to be immersed in the exploration of content themes that truly intrigue and engage them. Investigations into themes such as how plants grow, the many ways we travel, or the change of the seasons involve communication through listening, speaking, reading, and writing. A wide array of children's literature is available to support virtually any theme that teachers and children might wish to study. Teachers can read aloud to children and have them respond in various ways. They can involve children in shared reading and writing and in activities promoting phonemic awareness and phonics. The point here is that learning to read and write is a unifying element that touches every aspect of the curriculum. While discrete lessons on various aspects of literacy learning are important, opportunities to connect and apply the learning across curriculum content are what makes those lessons stick. A sound curriculum for young children is grounded in helping them use and build on what they know in the process of becoming self-reliant, independent learners.

LEADERSHIP STRATEGIES

Selecting a curriculum program model for implementation in your school is a very big decision. We suggest that leaders guide staff members to discuss what they believe about how children learn and how they are best taught before even looking at available curricula. For example, you may wish to consider whether or not you want a program that is highly prescriptive (scripted), detailing everything a teacher is to say and do. Or you may want a program that consists of a set of activities, loosely organized around a set of topics or curriculum areas. Further, you may look more favorably on programs that provide some structure and guidance for teachers with opportunities for teacher flexibility and decision making. Figure 5.1 offers a set of questions for early childhood educators to consider when adopting a curriculum model.

Within any curriculum, even the most well-intentioned, teachers may have difficulty meeting the challenges associated with children whose cultural and linguistic backgrounds differ from their own. Figure 5.2 is offered as a stimulus for candid and thoughtful discussions about the challenges faced by the entire school community—the children and their families, teachers, and administrators. Its use is intended to encourage a mutually supportive environment for all involved.

Informed educational leaders can tell a great deal about the quality of instruction in a classroom simply by observing the literacy environment. The checklist in Figure 5.3 is meant to serve as a reminder of the type of evidence on display where literacy learning is active and supported through the classroom learning environment.

FIGURE 5.1 Questions to Consider About a Proposed Curriculum Model

1. What is the theoretical orientation of the curriculum model?
    How does the theoretical model define the roles of the teacher and
    the child in initiating learning?

2. What domains of learning are addressed, and are they integrated or
    treated as distinctly separate content and skills?
    How much emphasis is placed on oral language development,
    higher-order thinking, and problem solving?
    Will the curriculum lead to achievement of state standards?

3. Does the curriculum model provide guidance, adaptations, and
    specific strategies to differentiate teaching depending on
    characteristics of the children (e.g., children with special
    needs, English Language Learners, children with challenging
    behaviors)?

4. How is learning assessed?
    Is an assessment system provided that is consistent with the teaching
    philosophy and content of the model?

5. What is the research base for this curriculum model?

Note: Adapted from Frede & Ackerman, 2006, p. 2.

Figure 5.2 Characteristics of Effective Schools and Classrooms for Linguistically and Culturally Diverse Preschool Children and Their Families

Throughout the **school**, teachers and administrators—

- Show sensitivity and respect for the diverse community of learners and families
- Demonstrate awareness that all parents have goals and aspirations for their children
- Make attempts to learn as much as possible about the children and their families
- Encourage parents to engage in extended conversation with their children
- Encourage parents to read to their children in whatever language they feel most comfortable

In **classrooms** with English Language Learners, teachers—

- Accompany verbal communication with lots of nonverbal communication and gestures
- Attempt to keep messages simple
- Focus lots of talk on the here and now
- Emphasize the important words in a sentence
- Encourage a low-risk environment for oral language use in any language
- Include some personal, extended conversations that go beyond the here and now
- Show respect for all languages while helping children expand their understanding and use of English

The appropriate use of technology is another aspect of the learning environment. When evaluating software for purchase, we recommend that teachers collaborate. Inquiries made to independent evaluators and other teachers will be of enormous help in making good decisions. The list of questions in Figure 5.4 is meant to serve as a reminder about some important points to consider.

Figure 5.3 Print-Rich Environment Checklist

___ 1.   Print is visible on open charts and bulletin boards around the room.

___ 2.   Children's names are printed on their cubbies, place mats, paintings, and other items.

___ 3.   Children are encouraged to write their own names or letters from their names on their paintings and drawings.

___ 4.   Environmental print is clear, easy to read, meaningful, and displayed at children's eye level.

___ 5.   Print in the environment represents words familiar to children through daily activities and through thematic inquiry about growing things, the neighborhood, and other special experiences.

___ 6.   Where appropriate, some print is written in languages other than English.

___ 7.   Name cards and other carefully printed words are available for children to copy or "read."

___ 8.   Functional uses of print are incorporated into the routine activities, for example:

- Mailboxes are available for each child/family to encourage the sharing of messages between home and school.

- A newsletter describing children's activities is shared with the children and sent home regularly.

___ 9.   Print is incorporated in every area of the classroom.

FIGURE 5.4 Questions to Consider When Evaluating Software Programs for Purchase

Questions Related to Curriculum Content

1. Is the content appropriate for the curriculum?

2. Does the program fulfill the educational outcomes it promises?

3. Are the educational strategies sound?

Questions Related to Student Use and Engagement

4. How much knowledge is needed to use the program?

5. How much student interaction is available?

6. Does the learner have control over navigation through the program?

7. Does the learner have control over the level of difficulty?

8. Does the learner have control over entering and exiting at any place in the program?

9. Can the learner use the program without help from an adult?

10. Is feedback appropriate for correct or incorrect responses?

11. Are graphics, animation, and sound used in an appropriate manner?

12. Do the graphics, animation, and sound enhance the learning experience?

Note: Adapted from Anderson & Speck, 2001.

CHAPTER 6

Accountability and Assessment

MONITORING AND ASSESSING children's early literacy development is an important part of a comprehensive early childhood program. Assessment has a number of purposes. It is used to monitor children's development and learning, to guide a teacher's planning and decision making, to identify children who might benefit from special services, and to report to and communicate with others (McAfee, Leong, & Bodrova, 2004). Helpful assessments reveal what children *can* do as well as what they cannot do.

It is useful to make the distinction between assessment and evaluation. Assessment is a procedure or set of procedures used to determine the degree to which an individual child possesses a certain attribute. Assessments may be formal or informal in nature. Academic readiness tests, developmental screening tests, and diagnostic tests are all types of formal assessments, and most are standardized tests. Informal assessments include such things as anecdotal records, portfolio assessment information, and developmental or academic checklists (Gullo, 2005). Evaluation is a process of making judgments about the merit, value, or worth of educational programs, materials, or techniques and may include judgments about a child's progress within a particular program relative to a set of expectations.

In addition to the ongoing, day-by-day assessments that link closely to the early childhood curriculum, there is a growing trend toward the use of child assessments for program accountability. These assessments, in which early literacy is often a major component, reflect an increasingly high-stakes climate in which preschool programs are required to demonstrate effectiveness (often in terms standardized measures) in improving school readiness and creating positive child outcomes. Information related to early literacy is sometimes interpreted as being representative of all aspects of the instructional program.

Many of today's early childhood programs make use of multiple methods of assessment, any of which may focus on early literacy development. These assessments include the following:

- *Screening instruments*—quick assessments designed to alert teachers to a problem in a specific area
- *Diagnostic assessments*—individually administered and designed to identify specific instructional needs after a problem has been identified
- *Progress-monitoring assessments*—closely linked to the curriculum and used to determine whether or not instruction is having the desired effect
- *Standardized tests* (or outcome tests)—nationally normed, group achievement tests and state-developed competency tests, which measure long-term growth and are useful for comparing groups rather than assessing individual progress

The growing use of outcome measures at the early childhood level reflects the downward extension of an increasingly high-stakes climate in K–12 education.

CONCERNS ABOUT EARLY LITERACY ASSESSMENT

Concerns about trends in early literacy assessment include the use of measures that focus on a limited range of skills and the very nature of the assessments in use. Both factors may cause teachers to narrow their curriculum and teaching practices, especially when the stakes are high. For example, the ability to name the letters of the alphabet is usually assessed in a decontextualized manner in which a child is asked to name each letter as it is presented, one at a time.

Unfortunately, this can lead to teaching in which the letters of the alphabet are only presented in a discrete and decontextualized manner apart from children's names or the application of that knowledge to other meaningful print. Although children may be capable of naming letters in a robotic-like, rote-memorization manner, they may fail to acquire the long-term goal—an understanding of how the letters function for reading and writing and the ability to use what they know to make sense of the print in their environment.

Another concern is the need for the development and use of reliable and valid measures of children's overall language development and background knowledge. The exclusive use of measures such as the Peabody Picture Vocabulary Test (Dunn & Dunn, 1997) to measure language development in major early childhood program models may inadvertently suggest to teachers that matching spoken words with pictures represents the entire range of receptive and expressive language abilities, and thus narrow teachers' mindset about what is important in the realm of oral language development. Attention to broadening children's background knowledge may also suffer. Inherent to an effective literacy program is the engagement of children in interesting content about which they can talk, read (or have read to them), write, and act. Systematic assessment in these areas might serve to focus teachers' attention on the development of children's listening and speaking abilities through the exploration of rich content of interest and importance to them (e.g., in science and social studies).

Additional concerns include the use of assessment instruments that may be more developmentally appropriate for older children and those that are not culturally or linguistically appropriate. "Sound assessment gives each child, regardless of that child's experience, status, or background, as good a chance as any other child to show what he or she knows and can do" (McAfee, Leong, & Bodrova, 2004, p. 11).

Ethical concerns regarding the misuse of assessment results have been raised by a number of groups (NAEYC & NAECS/SDE, 2003). McAfee, Leong, and Bodrova (2004) offer several ethical dos and don'ts, which are particularly relevant to the assessment of early literacy development:

1. *On multiple measures.* Use multiple measures if the assessment information will be the basis for important educational decisions and recommendations; never make such important decisions from just a single test.
2. *On screening.* Use standardized screening tests only for further evaluation. Link screenings to a follow-up that could provide needed services. Examine the validity and reliability of locally developed screening instruments and processes before they are used.
3. *On tracking.* Avoid the use of assessment results to form fixed ability or skill groups that track children and narrow their opportunities to learn.
4. *On tailoring instruction.* Use assessment results to individualize instruction so that it matches the child's current (not past) needs.

ASSESSMENT MEASURES

Checklists, anecdotal records, work samples, and portfolios are commonly used for classroom assessment. Observational assessment tools such as these are often termed performance-based assessments. Children are assessed in their natural environments as they perform actual tasks. As we have noted earlier, the use of standardized tests is increasing, as policy makers and educators seek objective measures of children's achievement and school readiness. Following is a brief description of several methods of assessment with some implications for their use.

Checklists

Checklists are lists of items describing behaviors related to a particular topic or developmental or curriculum area with places to check whether or not each behavior is present and perhaps to what degree. Checklists help teachers organize their observations of children's performance relative to specific goals and objectives. Information collected over time may be compared and used by teachers to draw conclusions about a child's progress and to make instructional decisions. Checklists can be made for virtually anything to be observed. In addition, many curriculum materials and professional resources include checklists for early language and literacy development, such as shown in Figure 6.1.

FIGURE 6.1 Selected Items on Checklist for Observing Young Children's Expressive Language Development

Language/Literacy Development	Observed	Not Observed
Responds when spoken to		
Takes turns speaking		
Speaks clearly		
Asks questions		
Participates in group discussions		
Tells personal stories		

Anecdotal Records

A collection of brief notes (anecdotes) made about something observed in a particular child is termed an *anecdotal record*. The notes may be based on observations during whole- or small-group instruction, or they may be recorded on the spot when working with the child one-to-one. Used along with other sources of information, anecdotes help provide a picture of a child's overall performance.

The following is an example of an anecdote:

Upon entering the classroom this morning, Jeffrey searched through the name cards on display for a very long time. He decided to choose Jeremy's name card to hold up when I call out each person's name for attendance. October 10

Work Samples

Samples of actual work done by a child may include drawings, paintings, attempts at writing, self-portraits, or anything that represents a product done in the classroom. Samples of work collected over a period of time can indicate the child's growth and are excellent to share with the child's family. Dated samples of a child's attempts to write his or her own name are particularly good to share with the child as evidence of personal growth and development.

The examples shown in Figure 6.2 show the progression of a child's writing over time. We found these work samples particularly significant because they were self-generated during play activities. According to Schickedanz and Casbergue (2004), these samples are a 4 year-old's grocery lists over time. In sample *a* we see some lines of scribble, but among the scribbles are distinct little forms, some of which are mock letters. In sample *b* there are many mock letters and a few actual letters *(A, R, V, and O)*. Sample *c* shows many actual letters and a few mock letters. When knowledgeable teachers collect and analyze work samples of this type, they get a sense of a child's development. They also have evidence to share and discuss with parents and administrators.

Porfolios

A compilation of the evidence of a child's learning, collected over time to demonstrate the child's efforts, progress, or achievement, is termed a *portfolio*. The work might be stored in a folder, box, or any other type of container devoted to the collection. The portfolio itself is not an assessment. Rather, it is a tool that assists teachers in systematically storing and displaying evidence from various types of assessments. Checklists, anecdotal records, work samples, and any other type of relevant and meaningful evidence may be included in the portfolio. There are many types of portfolios differentiated by what each includes:

- *Developmental (working) portfolios*—work samples that indicate student growth
- *Showcase portfolios*—work samples of "best work" selected by the teacher or child

FIGURE 6.2 From Mock Letters to Real Letters

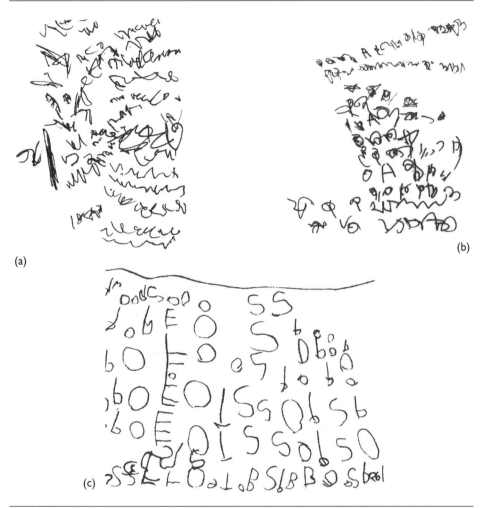

Note: Figure 6 (pg. 19) from Schickendanz, Judith A., & Casbergue, Renée M. (2004). *Writing in Preschool: Learning to Orchestrate Meaning and Marks*. Newark, DE: International Reading Association.

- *Record-keeping portfolios*—assessment information collected by the teacher
- *Cumulative portfolios*—representative work samples that follow students into subsequent grade levels

Literacy leaders may want to meet with teachers to see which type or combination of types of portfolios suits the needs of their situation. They should also discuss the methods by which teachers will interpret the information gathered. Obviously, it takes a well-informed professional to examine the material in a child's portfolio and make sense of it. Teachers look for developmental patterns and growth in terms of the expectations and standards set by the school or district. They look for indications of a child's personal growth over time as well. Portfolios are useful for reporting information about a child's progress to parents, administrators, and others who share responsibility for a child.

Standardized Tests

Assessments with prescribed methods for administration and scoring are termed *standardized tests*, or *outcome tests*. The conditions under which children are tested, such as time limits, directions, and actual testing circumstances, are meant to be the same whenever and wherever the test is given. Only the child's performance is meant to vary. Keeping test conditions constant is important if test results are to be compared across a population of children (norm-referenced tests) or with a set of criteria (criterion-referenced tests). The concerns raised earlier in this chapter about literacy assessment are particularly relevant to standardized tests. Educators worry about an apparent focus on a limited range of skills, developmental appropriateness of standardized tests, and their potential misuse. The concerns have made standardized tests very controversial in the early childhood community. Often called "high-stakes tests" because of their potential weight in decision making, standardized tests need to be well understood by leaders in early childhood literacy education.

LEADERSHIP STRATEGY

Early literacy leaders should be aware of a growing consensus about the need for some type of systematic documentation of children's development. As leaders they are expected to take a prominent role in planning and implementing an assessment program for their school. Figure 6.3 lists principles to consider in planning an assessment program.

FIGURE 6.3 Principles for Planning an Assessment Program

A sound program of assessment for early literacy development should

- Be linked to program standards and curriculum, which must be in place and well understood by all involved

- Address all areas of development (physical, social, emotional, cognitive); even though literacy is the assessment focus, all areas of development should be considered for potential links to problems or concerns

- Be systematic and ongoing over time in order to go beyond merely capturing snapshots of performance and to determine growth

- Be based on guidelines agreed upon by everyone involved about what and when to collect information and how to use it for planning instruction

- Make use of a variety of informal and formal tools and procedures (e.g., observational assessment methods such as anecdotal records, transcripts of conversations, reviews of drawings and writings, and checklists; when appropriate, limited use of standardized assessments by teachers or specialists to monitor progress)

- Occur during typical daily activities, providing a cross-check on curriculum since children should not be assessed on content or skills they do not have the opportunity to learn or demonstrate

- Demonstrate what a child can do independently without assistance

- Go beyond child outcomes to include systems for assessing professional development and parent involvement programs

CHAPTER 7

Leadership for Effective Professional Development

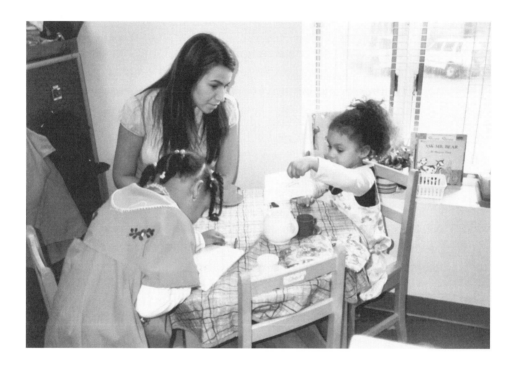

THE NEED FOR HIGHLY capable teachers is a constant theme in the literature on early childhood education. This is particularly true in the area of early literacy. National reports and government mandates have raised expectations for the formal education and training of early childhood teachers, especially in Head Start and in state-funded prekindergarten programs (National Research Council, 2001; U.S. Department of Health and Human Services, 2003). Today's early childhood teachers are expected to implement more challenging and effective curriculum in language and literacy and to assess and document progress in increasingly complex ways (National Research Council, 2001). Rising expectations coupled with an expanding number of early childhood programs have led to serious challenges in staffing, both in terms of the number of early childhood teachers and in the quality of their preparation.

Several states have established P–3 certification programs (New Jersey, Illinois, Ohio, Tennessee, and Massachusetts), with the goal of encouraging preservice teacher education majors to specialize in teaching young children. For those who are already teaching, many states have launched incentive efforts to encourage teachers and caregivers to upgrade and expand their knowledge and skills. These efforts may involve ongoing professional development for teachers, training for paraprofessionals, and teacher certification opportunities. Some initiatives are linked to compensation.

SETTING STANDARDS FOR TEACHERS OF EARLY LITERACY

Whether preservice or inservice, the demands regarding what early childhood teachers need to know and do have changed dramatically. Even those teachers who come from exemplary preservice programs will need continuing support. Described in broad terms, teachers of young children need to know the importance of oral language competencies, early literacy experiences, and family literacy in learning to read. They need to be able to foster a wide range of language- and literacy-related dispositions and competencies, including positive attitudes about reading and writing and the development of vocabulary, oral language (receptive and expressive) abilities, phonological awareness, and print-related knowledge. They must be able to use a variety of instructional methods that are age and developmentally appropriate and have the ability to adjust those methods to the specific needs of individual children. Teachers must be skilled in the ability to use multiple methods of monitoring children's literacy development and interpreting assessments in order to make sound instructional decisions.

An indication of the depth of knowledge expected of early childhood teachers is provided by the following list of teacher competencies in only one area of early literacy, as developed by the Connecticut State Department of Education (2000).

Effective teachers of early literacy understand the relationship between oral language and literacy:

1. They are knowledgeable about a variety of oral-language competences (e.g., vocabulary, phonological awareness, listening comprehension) and how these competencies play a role in learning to read;
2. They understand the differences between informal/conversational language and formal/literate language;
3. They recognize the importance of talking with children, and encouraging talk among children, in developing oral-language competencies;
4. They recognize the importance of reading to children in developing both oral-language competencies and print-related knowledge (e.g., basic print concepts);
5. They understand the basis for common speech-sound confusions that may affect reading and spelling;
6. They have knowledge about comprehension strategies and apply that knowledge in response to literature during reading aloud;
7. They understand the meaning and importance of children's "active construction of meaning";
8. They understand the meaning and importance of "emergent literacy";
9. They have knowledge about learning theory. (p. 72)

CHARACTERISTICS OF EFFECTIVE AND INEFFECTIVE PROFESSIONAL DEVELOPMENT

A review of recent literature that addresses professional development for teachers of early reading reveals considerable agreement about a number of the features of effective professional development programs (e.g., Duffy, 2004; International Reading Association, 2004; Learning First Alliance, 1998; Moats, Cunningham, Wurtzel, Silbert, & Furry, 2002; Strickland & Kamil, 2004). These features can also be applied to professional development at the early childhood level. *Effective* professional development programs in early literacy:

• Focus on a well-articulated purpose that is clear to all participants. Participants understand what they are to do with the knowledge they receive.

- Focus on the actual content to be taught and the curriculum to be used.
- Take place in the classrooms and schools where teachers work and where demonstrations of techniques and approaches will be applied.
- Involve everyone in a school, group of schools, or school district whose responsibilities relate to the program's purpose. This includes administrators and supervisors; teachers across age/grade levels and years of experience; special service providers; and English language specialists.
- Are consistent in message. Presenters and facilitators draw program content from the same research base and sources of information about best practices.
- Are implemented and sustained over time. They allot extended time for initial training and incorporate time for extensive follow-up with teachers in their classrooms.
- Provide participants with a variety of experiences. These include both small-group and individualized support with opportunities for discussion, analysis, reflection, and evaluation.
- Provide teachers with ready access to someone who can help them understand and apply the content of the program in their classrooms.
- Are led by individuals who are well prepared and have proven their ability to teach both adults and the content that is the focus of the program. Facilitators and coaches work together to keep their messages consistent and to identify problems and to address them quickly.
- Have mechanisms for measuring changes that occur in teacher practice and student performance.

In contrast to the above characteristics, Calderon and Minaya-Rowe (2003) offer the following list of features of professional development programs that yield poor results. *Ineffective* professional development is characterized by

- A series of one-shot workshops on the "fad of the moment" or the "guru of the day";
- Separation of bilingual from mainstream teachers;
- No follow-up or provision for teacher learning communities for teacher reflection after the inservice training;
- No attention given to an individual teacher's needs and levels of expertise;

- No attention given to the context and diversity of classrooms;
- Minimal ongoing support to teachers (no facilitators, coaches, researchers). (p. 185)

PROFESSIONAL DEVELOPMENT MODELS

It is essential for leaders to be at the forefront in establishing a sense of where the faculty and staff are, a vision for where they want to be, and a plan for how they might get there. Knowing something about the range of possibilities available for putting a plan of action in place is critical to successful leadership. Following are brief descriptions of a few professional development models. These may be combined in ways that suit the needs of your situation. The purpose here is to strengthen and support your leadership role with background knowledge we think would be helpful for making decisions about some possible courses of action.

Whole-School-Involvement Process

Though many models of professional development have emerged over the past years, the reality is that most professional development continues to be delivered through inservice workshops on one or two annual professional development days. At times the workshops may consist of a smorgasbord of offerings that may have little to do with teachers' perceptions of what they need. These one-shot opportunities are unlikely to hit the mark as genuine professional development.

As a first step toward a broader vision of professional development, many school districts have transformed the notion of the annual professional development day into a series of focused workshops, seminars, or meetings that reflect the interests and needs of a subset of teachers or of a particular school within a district. These workshops are characterized by collaborative planning by teachers and leadership personnel. They are generally based on a cycle of planning for no less than one year at a time. Participants define their learning needs, logistical considerations, and needed support. The activities in which they engage generally reflect small-group-inquiry models in which the participants set their own goals and agendas. Outside "experts" may or may not be used. When they are invited, outside experts are selected to address a particular recognized need of the group. The goal is to build a learning community that shares a common interest and works toward a shared vision for improved instruction. Efforts of this type often combine several models of professional development, such as faculty study groups, coaching, and personal improvement plans.

Faculty Study Groups

Faculty study groups may involve the whole faculty, or they may involve faculty at specific age/grade levels with similar goals (Murphy & Lick, 1998; Strickland, Ganske, & Monroe, 2002). New faculty might be involved in a study group during their first year of teaching. Faculty study groups may be used to support curricular and instructional innovations, integrate the school's instructional programs, target a school-wide instructional need, and monitor the impact of changes on students. Groups of 6–8 members or less seem to work best. The topic will determine who participates in a given group. Weekly hour-long meetings are often effective. Leadership at the meetings can be rotated. It is a good idea to establish a study group action plan, including

1. The specific needs that the group will investigate
2. How student change that results from the work of the study group will be ascertained
3. The resources the group will use

The action plan may be used periodically to evaluate the effectiveness of the study group.

Coaching

Many school districts are combining workshops and other forms of professional development with coaching. Coaching is based on the view that teacher education is an ongoing process involving rigorous preservice training and experiential opportunities with continued inservice professional development. Most coaching programs involve literacy education. Literacy coaches are teachers with special expertise and training, who provide continuing support and guidance to classroom teachers in order to improve classroom instruction. Coaching has many advantages.

It allows for more personalized attention to specific concerns. It fosters opportunities for action, observation, and reflection with a knowledgeable and interested other.

Personal Improvement Plans

Many directors and principals like to engage teachers in developing their own personal improvement plans. Such plans allow teachers to set personal goals for self-improvement. Teachers identify an area of need or interest, explain why they wish to explore that area, and develop an overall plan. Plans include a statement of purpose, a list of proposed activities, and a method for evaluation. The proposed activities are stated in concrete terms and written so that someone with a similar background would be able to understand and carry them out. Most plans extend over one year. Periodic meetings are held between administrator and teacher to revisit the plan, discuss progress, and provide supportive mentoring where needed.

LEADERSHIP STRATEGIES

Many educators believe that now is the time for professional development to take a front seat along with standards and assessment as key elements of reform and research. The education climate has changed. The demand for high-quality literacy education for all children is, no doubt, here to stay. Achieving this goal will require high-quality, ongoing professional development for teachers. Effective leadership is essential to making it happen. Figure 7.1 offers some ideas to think about in planning for professional development.

The time spent by a literacy leader in planning and monitoring the process of professional development is likely to set everyone on track and keep them there in a positive and productive manner. Figure 7.2 can be used to help guide the ongoing work of a professional development effort. To illustrate its use, the chart has been completed with an example of the goal "Improve Vocabulary Instruction." You may wish to adapt the chart to meet your needs, such as adding more columns.

Figure 7.1 Planning for Effective Professional Development: A Checklist

Collaborate with staff to evaluate the current professional development activities in your school. Use the checklist below to project a long-term plan for ongoing, high-quality professional development.

- Develop a system for collecting the expressed needs of teachers. Create your own list of issues and concerns you perceive to need attention. Discuss and use both lists to develop the content focus.

- Throughout the planning, give attention to the learning context and diversity of the student population.

- Actively involve everyone in the planning process and as stakeholders in the outcome.

- Plan for and provide adequate time for staff to meet on a regular basis and for follow-up in specific classrooms where appropriate.

- Link professional development activities to the real day-by-day experiences of staff and children, using actual standards, curriculum materials, and assessments, including anecdotal records of student work.

- Provide opportunities for staff to work with those with similar age/grade responsibilities, as well as those whose responsibilities link with, but essentially differ from, their own.

- Project the plan over at least 1 year. Include plans for evaluation and continuation with suggested modifications for the future.

- Plan for an evaluation process in advance, making sure that everyone is aware of expectations.

FIGURE 7.2 Sample Professional Development Planning Guide

Overall Goal: Example—Improve Vocabulary Instruction

Specific Objectives	Professional Development Strategies	Participants	Time Line	Resources	Evidence
Focus on improved vocabulary instruction during read-aloud time, interactive reading, through thematic units.	Study groups read articles; collect, share, try out strategies. Workshops. Classroom observations; videotaping.	Teachers in Pre-K and K; the literacy coach.	Will divide year into parts to focus on each area of concern.	Technical assistance—literacy coach and faculty member from local college. Subscription to professional journals. Purchase of children's literature.	Teacher logs to document changes; teacher surveys; periodic analysis of classroom observations and videotapes; anecdotal records of students' vocabulary use in the classroom.

CHAPTER 8

Home–School Connections

T HE LINK BETWEEN supportive parental involvement and children's early literacy development is well established. Researchers have shown that children from homes where parents model the uses of literacy and engage children in activities that promote basic understandings about literacy are better prepared for school (Hart & Risley, 1995; Snow, Barnes, Chandler, Goodman, & Hemphill, 1991). Several national efforts such as Reading Is Fundamental and Reach Out and Read have focused with some success on getting books into the hands of parents and children and promoting regular parent–child book reading. Tabors,

Snow, and Dickinson (2001) report that efforts such as these have evidently worked to some extent, citing national surveys showing an increase in parent–child literacy activities among families with preschoolers. Unfortunately, however, the increases among families considered to be at greater risk lagged behind those of other families. These researchers recommend that efforts to promote shared reading with children go beyond giving books to families and include suggestions for how parents might use these activities to promote conversation and dialogue. They go further to suggest that it is not the frequency of book reading or even the quality of the talk that accompanies book reading alone that is related to children's language and literacy abilities, but the broader pattern of parent–child activities and interactions that support children's language and literacy development. The challenge is to get the message across to all parents, and particularly to low-income and low-education parents, that everyday activities of all sorts, accompanied by interesting talk with lots of new vocabulary words, can play an important part in their children's language and literacy development (Tabors et al., 2001).

PARENT INVOLVEMENT IN LANGUAGE AND LITERACY DEVELOPMENT

Parent education is an integral component of virtually all early childhood programs. However, its effectiveness varies widely. More and better research is needed to help us understand what kinds of parent involvement programs are most effective for certain target populations and at what level treatment intensity, training of providers, and attention to other program components is required (Barnett, 1998; St. Pierre & Layzer, 1998). Successful parent involvement programs help parents understand the importance of their role as "first teachers" and equip them with the skills and strategies to foster their children's language and literacy development. Key among the understandings that schools can help promote among parents are

1. The knowledge that a child's capacity for learning is not determined at birth and there is a great deal parents and caregivers can do to enhance it (Shonkoff & Phillips, 2000)

2. An awareness that there are many informal and enjoyable ways that language and literacy skills can be developed in the home
3. A recognition of the need to provide opportunities for children to use what they know about language and literacy in order to help them transfer what they know to new situations

Family Literacy Programs

The concept of family literacy is well established in both the literature on early childhood education and in practice. The concept has become most visible through government programs such as Head Start and Even Start. Through these programs, family literacy has been defined in terms of four components:

1. Interactive literacy activities between parents and their children
2. Training for parents on how to be their children's primary teacher and how to be full partners in the education of their children
3. Parent literacy training
4. Early childhood education, prekindergarten through primary grades

The definition translates into the provision of three core services to all families: parenting education, adult basic education, and the education of young children, with some activities provided with parents and children together and some instructional components taking place in the home (U.S. Department of Education, 1996). Certainly not all early childhood programs will be able to provide the full range of services described above. However, all can benefit from what has been learned from the work of national family literacy program efforts. The following list of defining characteristics that make family literacy programs successful emerged from a national symposium (U.S. Department of Education, 1996).

Effective family literacy programs

- offer literacy development for parents and children;
- serve as an extension of the family, recognizing their individual differences;

- include strong participant involvement;
- coordinate support services and other sources of funding;
- establish a designated time and a process for a parent support system;
- include parent–child interaction;
- integrate learning and participation on three levels: parents, children, and parent–child;
- integrate core instructional components, total program services, and staff development;
- offer ongoing monitoring of quality by all stakeholders;
- define family broadly—intergenerational, including children and caregiver(s);
- offer program goals that consider other support systems and agencies and offer links to other services; and
- address long-term student goals. (p. 11)

Efforts for Linking Home and School

Effective family literacy involvement programs depend on informed leadership. Most early childhood literacy programs have a variety of ongoing efforts in place to foster communication with parents, caregivers, and the community. These may include

- A parent or community advisory council
- A system for soliciting parent input for educational offerings, school safety, and planning meetings
- A system for borrowing books and other materials to be used at home
- Regular well-planned parents' meetings
- Opportunities for parents to selectively observe classrooms

Such programs have relationships with community groups, including neighborhood service organizations. Perhaps the most significant consideration for linking home and school is the realization by both that they are more likely to produce the desired outcomes for children when they operate in ways that are mutually supportive and demonstrate shared knowledge and a sense of purpose.

LITERACY STRATEGIES

Parent workshops are among the most common strategies for getting families involved in their children's learning. Indeed, well-planned and executed parent workshops allow parents and school faculty to learn from one another.

Any one of the statements in the checklist in Figure 8.1 could be used as the basis for discussion at a parent workshop. The items in the list all relate to parents' involvement in their child's language and literacy development. The entire checklist could be used during a workshop as the focus of discussion with open dialogue about the issues raised.

FIGURE 8.1 A Checklist of Statements for Parents to Think About and Discuss

Directions for Parents: Each of the following statements addresses something very important to your child's language and literacy development. Think about how your family is addressing each statement. Share some of the challenges you face. Share some of the ways you have managed to overcome some challenges.

1. I read aloud to my child often. We have an established routine that provides time for shared reading daily.

2. My child has seen me and other adults in the family read frequently.

3. There are books, magazines, and newspapers in our home.

4. We visit the library on a regular basis for story hour and for borrowing books.

5. My child has books of his or her own and a place to keep them.

6. I purchase books as gifts for my child.

7. Our conversations go beyond daily functions like eating, dressing, and bathing. We talk about the day's events and our experiences on local trips and activities.

8. I monitor the amount and quality of the television programs watched by my child.

9. I provide plenty of writing materials, such as paper, pencils and crayons, a chalkboard and chalk, for play activities.

10. I convey a positive attitude towards schools and teachers.

11. My child's hearing and vision are checked regularly.

12. I make sure that my child receives a balanced, healthy diet and gets the proper amount of rest.

Ask parents to think about the statements in the list. Encourage them to share how they cope with the challenges related to each. Be prepared with a few suggestions of your own for helping parents meet the challenges that go along with being busy parents with limited resources. You might wish to discuss each statement, one at a time, during one meeting. Or spread the discussion over several meetings during the year, discussing two or three statements at a time.

Once a topic is selected, planning a workshop goes well beyond sending out notices and providing refreshments. A possible template for planning parent workshops might include an initiating prompt to invite participation and get things started, time for participant response and interaction, and a planned wrap-up that serves to help participants summarize and reflect on what was discussed and provide a stimulus for them to make a mental or verbal commitment for follow-up. Figure 8.2 offers a more complete outline for planning.

FIGURE 8.2 A Template for Planning Family Literacy Activities

Before the Session

Select a particular goal or outcome on which to focus. For example:

- Reading aloud to your child
- Monitoring television viewing
- Engaging your child in extended conversations

Some Ground Rules

- Involve families and teachers in the planning
- Build on the cultural and linguistic backgrounds of participants
- Make use of multicultural, multilingual materials
- Give plenty of notice for meetings; then send a reminder
- Provide baby-sitting service and refreshments
- Prepare resource materials in advance

I. Introducing the Session

Use an "initiating prompt" to get attention and to illustrate the goal of the session. Some examples:

- Question or request

  Ex. "Share one thing you like best about your child and one thing that you and your child are working to improve."

- Videotape
- Demonstration (someone modeling a particular activity)

  Ex. a parent–child read-aloud; use of wordless books; a parent–child cooking experience

- Book talks on appropriate books for particular age groups; acquaint parents with the vast array of types of children's books (informational books, ABC, storybooks, etc.)

II. Participant Interaction

Guided discussion and hands-on activities
Participants actively engage in the session through

- Discussion
- Role-playing an activity
- Anything else that keeps their attention and allows them to participate fully

III. Wrap-up

Summarization and commitment
Participants contribute by

- Reflecting on the session and the desired outcomes
- Sharing what they found valuable and how they plan to act on it

Workshop leader(s) facilitates by

- Also suggesting ways that parents might act on what was discussed
- Distributing and discussing resource materials
- Engaging participants in planning for follow-up session

CHAPTER 9

Early Childhood Leaders as Advocates for Children

TODAY'S LITERACY LEADERS often act as advocates for better public policy regarding early childhood education, including early literacy. They interact with boards of education, local government representatives, state legislators, and other policy makers. They share responsibility for providing accurate information to those who enact policy decisions regarding the standards and resources that affect their programs. The outlines below of *What We Know* with accompanying *Policy Recommendations* were first published in a policy brief prepared for the National Institute for Early Education Research (NIEER; Strickland & Riley-Ayers, 2006). It is provided here as a resource of key ideas that might be used to advocate for improved early literacy programs. Each point is based on key findings from the research on early literacy.

WHAT WE KNOW

- Literacy development starts early in life and is highly correlated with school achievement.
- All of the domains of a child's development—physical, social–emotional, cognitive, language, and literacy—are interrelated and interdependent.
- The more limited a child's experiences with language and literacy, the more likely he or she will have difficulty learning to read.
- Key early literacy predictors of reading and school success include oral language (listening and vocabulary development), alphabetic code (phonological/phonemic awareness and alphabet knowledge), and print knowledge.
- Well-conceived standards for child outcomes, curriculum content, and teacher preparation help establish clarity of purpose and a shared vision for early literacy education.
- Increased demands for program accountability are often heavily focused on assessments of children's early literacy development.
- Highly capable teachers are required to implement today's more challenging early literacy curriculum.
- Teacher knowledge, respect, and support for the diversity of children's families, cultures, and linguistic backgrounds are important factors in early literacy development.

POLICY RECOMMENDATIONS

- All children should have access to early childhood programs with strong literacy components that include clear adaptations for children with special needs.
- Early literacy curricula and teaching practices should be evidence-based, integrated with all domains of learning, and understandable to staff members.

- States and districts should establish standards for early literacy that are articulated with K-12 programs and reflect consistency and continuity with overall program goals.
- Early literacy assessment should use multiple means of collecting and synthesizing information and use the information to improve both teaching and the total preschool program.
- Standards for early childhood professionals should require that staff members are qualified to meet early literacy instructional standards.
- Parent involvement programs should have a strong early literacy component that guides parents and caregivers in providing early literacy experiences at home.
- Support for English Language Learners must be specified and provided both in the home language and in English where feasible.

Resources

Assessment

Jones, J. (2004). Framing the assessment discussion. *Young Children, 59*(1), 14–18.

> This article informs educators about the distinctions between testing and the process of assessment. It poses several questions that help to structure discussions about accountability and testing.

McAfee, O., Leong, D. J., & Bodrova, E. (2004). *Basics of assessment: A primer for early childhood educators.* Washington, DC: NAEYC.

> This is a clearly written book describing the types of assessments in use today in early childhood programs. It also discusses using assessment information and offers cautions regarding misuses of assessments. Examples illustrate the text throughout.

National Association for the Education of Young Children & National Association of Early Childhood Specialists in State Departments of Education. (2003). *Early childhood curriculum, assessment, and program evaluation.* Washington, DC: NAEYC. Online: http://www.naeyc.org/about/positions/cape.asp

> This position statement offers educators useful information about three important topics: curriculum, assessment, and program evaluation. A supplement on screening and assessment of young English Language Learners is also available.

Child Development and Early Literacy Learning

International Reading Association (IRA) & National Association for the Education of Young Children (NAEYC). (1998). Learning to read and write: Developmentally appropriate practices for young children. A joint position statement of the IRA and NAEYC. *Young Children, 53*(4), 30–46. Online: www.naeyc.org/about/positions/pdf/PSREAD98.PDF.

> This position statement provides educators with a look at the development of the young child and a look at effective instruction divided in three sections: birth through preschool, kindergarten, and the primary grades.

Nekovei, D. L., & Ermis, S. A. (2006). Creating classrooms that promote rich vocabularies for at-risk learners. *Young Children, 61*(5), 90–95.

> Vocabulary development is highly related to early literacy achievement. This article provides a practical discussion of the many ways that good early care and education programs can support and expand children's vocabularies. Suggestions for providing meaningful, rich language opportunities in the classroom are offered.

Roskos, K. A., Christie, J. F., & Richgels, D. J. (2003). The essentials of early literacy instruction. *Young Children, 58*(2), 52–59.

> This informative article provides information about the content of early literacy instruction as well as the dispositions of early literacy instruction. It clearly outlines eight early literacy teaching strategies for educators to use in the classroom.

Curriculum

International Reading Association. (1998). *Phonemic awareness and the teaching of reading: A position statement from the board of directors of the International Reading Association.* Newark, DE: Author. Online: http://www.reading.org/downloads/positions/ps1025_phonemic.pdf

> This pamphlet provides much-needed clarification of phonemic awareness in a clear and concise manner. It provides a definition, information about its development, and what it means for classroom practice.

Schickedanz, J. A., & Casbergue, R. M. (2004). *Writing in preschool: Learning to orchestrate meaning and marks.* Newark, DE: IRA.

> As part of a Preschool Literacy Collection, this book provides a thorough look at the development of student writing and highlights the role of materials and adult involvement in its development.

Strickland, D. S., & Schickedanz, J. A. (2004). *Learning about print in preschool: Working with letters, words, and beginning links with phonemic awareness.* Newark, DE: IRA.

> This useful and practical book provides a comprehensive look at print in preschool as part of the Preschool Literacy Collection. It supplies educators with background knowledge about the connection of child development and learning about print and clearly outlines focused strategies for use in the classroom in developing concepts of print, phonemic awareness, and alphabet knowledge.

Vukelich, C., & Christie, J. (2004). *Building a foundation for preschool literacy: Effective instruction for children's reading and writing development.* Newark, DE: IRA.

> This easy-to-read book is part of the Preschool Literacy Collection and focuses specifically on instruction, including creating a literacy-rich environment, planning the daily schedule, standards and assessment, and working with parents.

English Language Learners

Okagaki, L., & Diamond, K. E. (2000). Responding to cultural and linguistic differences in the beliefs and practices of families with young children. *Young Children, 55*(3), 74–80.

> This article provides the reader with a wealth of knowledge regarding the differences in beliefs and practices across cultures. The authors illustrate these differences in relation to children's experience in early childhood settings. They also provide valuable implications for teachers and caregivers and offer suggestions for developing sensitivity to parents' beliefs and practices.

Ready at Five Partnership. (2004). *What works? Promising practices for improving the school readiness of English language learners.* Baltimore, MD: Author.

> This document offers educators a broad look at English Language Learners. It provides critical elements for success and gives readers a concrete look at the effective practices or critical elements through snapshots of implementation at specific locations.

Tabors, P. O. (1997). *One child, two languages: A guide for preschool educators of children learning English as a second language.* Baltimore, MD: Brookes.

> This valuable book provides preschool educators a practical reference that presents background knowledge about second language learning. It also offers meaningful and useful strategies for the classroom to support second language learning in young children.

Tabors, P. O., & Snow, C. E. (2001). Young bilingual children and early literacy development. In S. B. Neuman & D. K. Dickinson (Eds.), *Handbook of early literacy research* (pp.159–178). New York: Guilford.

> This book chapter provides an extensive look at bilingual children from birth to age 8. It provides a comprehensive section on early care and education settings for children ages 3–5. In this section the authors share research that looks at three types of classrooms: the first-language classroom (all-English or all-first-language-other-than-English), the bilingual classroom, and the English-language classroom.

Home–School Connections

Burningham, L. M., & Dever, M. T. (2005). An interactive model for fostering family literacy. *Young Children, 60*(5), 87–94.

> This article describes a family literacy project that provided an early childhood literacy program for parents. The project engaged parents in reading with their children and provided explicit instruction in effective ways to do this.

Ordonez-Jasis, R., & Ortiz, R. W. (2006). Reading their worlds: Working with diverse families to enhance children's early literacy development. *Young Children, 61*(1), 42–48.

> This article offers eight recommendations to promote culturally sensitive family literacy programs.

Leadership

Carton, C. E., & Groves, M. M. (1999). Teacher to director: A developmental journey. *Early Childhood Education Journal, 26*(3), 183–188.

> This article outlines the similarities and differences between teaching and directing roles. It also leads the reader through the stages of growth for administrators that lead to a self-awareness and professional growth. Lastly, it emphasizes professional development plans for administration to ensure growth opportunities.

Kagan, S., & Bowman, B. (Eds.). (1997). *Leadership in early care and education.* Washington, DC: NAEYC.

> This book offers leaders support in such areas as mentoring, effective management, and becoming a leader in the community. It has chapters that outline the challenges of leadership and new directions in fostering leadership in early childhood.

Rodd, J. (1998). *Leadership in early childhood: The pathway to professionalism.* New York: Teachers College Press.

> This book guides the early childhood leader through such topics as conflict resolution, building and leading a team, partnering with parents and the public, and initiating and implementing change.

Taba, S., Castle, A., Vermeer, M., Hanchett, K., Flores, D., & Caufield, R. (1999). Lighting the path: Developing leadership in early education. *Early Childhood Education Journal, 26*(3), 173–177.

> In this article the authors outline lessons learned and calls to action in advocacy leadership, administrative leadership, community leadership, conceptual leadership, and career development leadership.

Professional Development

Bloom, P. (2002). *Making the most of meetings: A practical guide*. Washington, DC: NAEYC.

> This guide shows early childhood leaders how to effectively run staff meetings. It offers suggestions to make the meetings more efficient, engaging, and productive.

National Association for the Education of Young Children. (1993). *A conceptual framework for early childhood professional development*. Washington, DC: Author. Online: http://www.naeyc.org/about/positions/pdf/psconf98.pdf

> This paper offers nine principles of effective professional development and tackles the issue of linking professional development and compensation.

Strickland, D. S., & Kamil, M. L. (Eds.). (2004). *Improving reading achievement through professional development*. Norwood, MA: Christopher-Gordon.

> This edited book is a compilation of contributions from well-known researchers in the field of literacy that provide a thorough look at professional development. It examines teacher preparation, professional development across instructional levels, and issues in professional development, and provides short descriptions of professional development ideas that make a difference.

Standards

Gronlund, G. (2006). *Make early learning standards come alive: Connecting your practice and curriculum to state guidelines*. Washington, DC: NAEYC.

> This valuable resource provides clear support in planning curriculum with learning standards in a developmentally appropriate way. It additionally provides guidance in assessing students' progress toward the standards. It offers a look not only at literacy, but also at other areas including mathematics, creative arts, and physical development.

Kagan, S. L., & Scott-Little, C. (2004). Early learning standards: Changing the parlance and practice of early childhood education? *Phi Delta Kappan, 85*(5), 388–396.

> This article gives an overview of new directions in the development and use of standards in early childhood education. It provides the how and why early learning standards emerged as well as some challenges that lie ahead.

National Association for the Education of Young Children & National Association of Early Childhood Specialists in State Departments of Education. (2002). *Early learning standards: Creating the conditions for success.* Washington, DC: NAEYC. Online: http://www.naeyc.org/about/positions/learning_standards.asp

>   This document provides educators with a thorough description of four essential features of effective early learning standards.

Seefeldt, C. (2005). *How to work with standards in the early childhood classroom.* New York: Teachers College Press.

>   This helpful guide offers leaders background knowledge to help them work with standards, use them effectively, and assess students' progress toward them.

Teachers of English to Speakers of Other Languages. (1997). *ESL standards for pre-K–12 students.* Alexandria, VA: Author.

>   Contains ESL standards organized into grade-level clusters: pre-K, K–3, 4–8, and 9–12. Each standard is explicated by descriptors, sample progress indicators, and classroom vignettes with discussion.

Glossary
of Literacy
Education Terms

The number in parentheses represents the chapter(s) in which the term is discussed in the text.

GENERAL TERMS

Alphabet knowledge: The ability to identify the 26 letters of the alphabet. (2, 4)

Concept of letter: The understanding that letters have distinct shapes, have names, and form words. (4)

Concepts of print: Children's understandings about the functions (e.g., practical uses), structure (e.g., printed words are separated by spaces), and conventions (e.g., left-to-right, top-to-bottom sequence) of written language. (4)

Differentiated instruction: The provision of varied learning situations, as whole-class, small-group, or individual instruction, to meet the varied needs of students. (5)

Environmental print: The print children see around them. This includes purposeful print such as stop signs and labels on food containers and other products, and signs in locations such as fast food restaurants. (4)

Fine motor development: The use of small muscles of the fingers and hands necessary for such tasks as picking up objects, writing, drawing, and managing buttons on clothes. (2)

Gross motor development: Control of the large muscles needed for movements like running, jumping, and climbing. (2)

Invented spelling: An attempt to spell a word whose spelling is not already known, based on knowledge of the spelling system and how it works. (2)

Onset: The part of a syllable that precedes the vowel, the initial consonant(s). For example, in one-syllable words, the *b* in *bump,* the *sh* in *shut,* or the *spl* in *splash.* Not all syllables have onsets—for example, *it, an.* (4)

Phoneme: The smallest unit in language; individual sounds. (2, 4)

Phonemic awareness: The ability to hear, identify, and manipulate the individual sounds (phonemes) in spoken words. (4)

Phonics: A way of teaching reading that stresses symbol–sound relationships, relating the sounds to letters that represent them. (4)

Phonological awareness: The ability to identify and make oral rhymes, to identify and work with syllables in spoken words, and to hear, identify, and manipulate the individual sounds— phonemes—in spoken words. (2, 4)

Rime: The vowel and any consonants that follow it in a syllable. In the words *sat* and *flat* the rime is *at.* (4)

Scaffolding: The process whereby a child's learning occurs in the context of full performance as adults gradually relinquish support. (2, 5)

Scientifically based research: A term used across a variety of fields, including medicine and education, to signal a set of key research characteristics designed to ensure that those who use the research can have a high degree of confidence that it is valid and dependable. (4)

Self-regulation: Evaluating and adjusting actions based on the potential or actual outcome of decisions. (2)

Sensory-perceptual development: The ability to receive information that comes through the senses and to recognize and interpret it. (2)

Shared reading: A classroom strategy in which a teacher reads a chart or book with enlarged print (big book) and encourages the children to read along on parts that they can remember or predict. Shared reading models the reading process and draws children's attention to print concepts and letter knowledge. (4)

Shared writing: A classroom strategy in which the teacher invites children to collaborate in the composing process. The teacher does the actual writing and guides the children to make suggestions about what should be included. The written text is based on a shared experience. (4)

Skill: An acquired ability to perform well; proficiency. (5)

Strategy: A systematic plan for solving a problem. (5)

Zone of proximal development (ZPD): The level at which a child finds a task too difficult to complete alone but achievable with the assistance of an adult or more experienced peer. (2)

TERMS RELATED TO ASSESSMENT

Anecdotal records: A collection of brief notes (anecdotes) recorded about something observed in a particular child. (6)

Benchmarks: Clearly outlined descriptions of knowledge or a skill for children to develop, used as a point of reference. (3, 6)

Checklists: Lists of items (behaviors) related to a particular topic or developmental or curriculum area with a place to check whether or not each behavior is present and sometimes to what degree it is present. (6)

Diagnostic assessments: Individually administered assessments designed to identify specific instructional needs after a problem has been identified. (6)

Observational assessment: A process in which a teacher systematically observes and records information about a child's knowledge, skills, strategies, and attitudes to determine what has been learned and to support progress. (6)

Performance-based assessment: An assessment that examines a child in his or her natural environment performing actual tasks. (6)

Portfolio assessment: A compilation of the evidence of a child's learning, collected over time, that demonstrates the child's efforts, progress, and achievement. Types of portfolios include:

Cumulative portfolios: Representative work samples that follow students in subsequent grade levels. (6)

Developmental (working) portfolios: Work samples that indicate student growth. (6)

Record-keeping portfolios: Assessment information collected by the teacher. (6)

Showcase portfolios: Work samples of "best work" selected by the teacher or child. (6)

Progress-monitoring assessments: Measures closely aligned to the curriculum and used to determine whether or not instruction is having the desired effect. (6)

Screening instruments: Quick assessments designed to alert teachers to a problem in a specific area. (6)

Standardized tests (outcome tests): Nationally normed group achievement tests and state-developed competency tests that measure long-term growth and are useful for comparing groups rather than assessing individual progress. (6)

Work samples: Samples of actual work done by a child. May include drawings, paintings, attempts at writing, self-portraits, or anything that represents a product done in the classroom. (6)

TERMS RELATED TO EARLY LEARNING STANDARDS

Standards: Specifications of curriculum content, operational guidelines for programs and classroom instruction, and child outcomes. Types of standards include

Child-outcome standards: Expectations for children's learning at the end of a given period of time. (3)

Classroom standards: Identification of classroom characteristics such as the maximum number of children and the materials and supports available to children and families. (3)

Program standards: The set of guidelines that direct program operation and instruction. (3)

Teaching and curriculum standards: Guidelines for the establishment of goals for the content that children are expected to learn, the planned activities, daily schedule and routines linked to these goals, and the availability and use of materials for children. (3)

References

Allen, K. E., & Marotz, L. (1994). *Developmental profiles: Birth to six.* Albany, NY: Delmar.

Anderson, R. S., & Speck, B. (2001). *Using technology in K–8 literacy classrooms.* Upper Saddle River, NJ: Merrill Prentice Hall.

Armbruster, B. B., Lehr, F., & Osborn, J. (2001). *Put reading first: The research building blocks for teaching children to read.* Washington, DC: Partnership for Reading.

Barnett, W. S. (1998). Long-term effects on cognitive development and school success. In W. S. Barnett & S. Boocock (Eds.), *Early care and education for children in poverty* (pp. 11–44). Albany: State University of New York Press.

Barnett, W. S. (2002). Preschool education for economically disadvantaged children: Effects on reading achievement and related outcomes. In S. Neuman & D. K. Dickinson (Eds.), *Handbook of early literacy research* (pp. 421–443). New York: Guilford.

Bowman, B., Donovan, M. S., & Burns, M. S. (Eds.). (2000). *Eager to learn: Educating our preschoolers.* Washington, DC: National Academy Press.

Calderon, M., & Minaya–Rowe, L. (2003). *Staff development and teacher learning communities: A step–by-step guide for administrators, teachers, and parents.* Thousand Oaks, CA: Corwin.

Cazden, C. (1988). *Classroom discourse.* Portsmouth, NH: Heinemann.

Clay, M. (1975). *The early detection of reading difficulties.* London: Heinemann.

Colorado State Department of Education. (2003). *Building blocks to Colorado's content standards: Reading and writing.* Retrieved November 20, 2005, from http://www.cde.state.co.us/earlychildhoodconnections/pdf/building_blocks4-26.pdf

Connecticut State Department of Education. (2000). *Connecticut's blueprint for reading achievement.* Hartford, CT: Author.

Dickinson, D., & Tabors, P. (2001). *Beginning literacy with language.* Baltimore, MD: Brookes.

Duffy, G. G. (1993). Rethinking strategy instruction: Four teachers' development and their low achievers. *The Elementary School Journal, 93,* 231–247.

Duffy, G. G. (2004). Teachers who improve reading achievement: What research says about what they do and how to develop them. In D. S. Strickland & M. L. Kamil (Eds.), *Improving reading achievement through professional development* (pp. 3–22). Norwood, MA: Christopher Gordon.

Duke, N. K., Pressley, M., & Hilden, K. (2004). Assessment of reading comprehension. In C. A. Stone, E. R. Silliman, B. J. Ehren, & K. Apel (Eds.), *Handbook of language and literacy: Development and disorders* (pp. 521–540). New York: Guilford.

Dunn, L., & Dunn, L. (1997). *Peabody picture vocabulary test–3.* Circle Pines, MN: American Guidance Service.

Frede, E., & Ackerman, D. J. (2006). *Curriculum decision making: Dimensions to consider.* New Brunswick, NJ: NIEER. Retrieved July 22, 2006, from http://nieer.org/resources/research/CurriculumDecisionMaking.pdf

Gullo, D. F. (2005). *Understanding assessment and evaluation in early childhood education* (2nd ed.). New York: Teachers College Press.

Halliday, M. A. K. (1969). Relevant models of language. *Educational Review, 22,* 26–37.

Hamre, B. K., & Pianta, R. C. (2005). Can instructional and emotional support in first-grade classrooms make a difference for children at risk of school failure? *Child Development, 76,* 949–967.

Hart, B., & Risely, T. R. (1995). *Meaningful differences in the everyday experience of young American children.* Baltimore, MD: Brookes.

Howes, C., & Tonyan, H. A. (2000). Links between adult and peer relationships across four developmental periods. In K. A. Kerns & A. M. Neal-Barnett (Eds.), *Examining associations between parent-child and peer relationships* (pp. 85–113). New York: Greenwood/Praeger.

International Reading Association. (2003). *Standards for reading professionals.* Newark, DE: Author.

International Reading Association. (2004). *The role and qualifications of the reading coach in the United States: A position statement of the International Reading Association.* Newark, DE: Author.

International Reading Association & National Association for the Education of Young Children. (1998). *Learning to read and write: Developmentally appropriate practices for young children.* Newark, DE: IRA.

Juel, C. (1988). Learning to read and write: A longitudinal study of 34 children from first through fourth grades. *Journal of Educational Psychology, 80,* 437–447.

Justice, L. M., & Pullen, P. C. (2003). Promising interventions for promoting emergent literacy skills: Three evidence-based approaches.

Topics in Early Childhood Special Education, 23, 99–113.

Kendall, J. S., & Marzano, R. J. (2004). *Content knowledge: A compendium of standards and benchmarks for K–12 education.* Aurora, CO: Mid-continent Research for Education and Learning (McREL). Online database: http://www.Mcrel.org/standards-benchmarks

Learning First Alliance. (1998). *Every child reading: An action plan.* Washington, DC: Author. Available online at http://www.read-bygrade3.com/1fa.htm

Louisiana State Department of Education. (2003). *Louisiana standards for programs serving four-year-old children: Bulletin 105.* Retrieved November 20, 2005, from http://www.doe.state.la.us/lde/uploads/3014.pdf

McAfee, O., Leong, D. J., & Bodrova, E. (2004). *Basics of assessment: A primer for early childhood educators.* Washington, DC: NAEYC.

Missouri Department of Elementary and Secondary Education Early Childhood Section. (n.d.). *Missouri pre–K literacy standards.* Retrieved November 20, 2005, from http://dese.mo.gov/divimprove/fedprog/earlychild/PreK_Standards/Literacy_Standards.pdf

Moats, L. C., Cunningham, A., Wurtzel, J., Silbert, J., & Furry, A. (2002). *Professional development for teachers of reading (slide presentation).* Retrieved July 18, 2006, from http://www.nifl.gov/partnershipfor-reading/presentations/reading_leadership.html

Morrow, L. M., & Schickedanz, J. A. (2006). The relationship between sociodramatic play and literacy development. In D. K. Dickinson & S. B. Neuman (Eds.), *Handbook of early literacy: Vol. 2* (pp. 269–280). New York: Guilford.

Murphy, C. U., & Lick, D. W. (1998). *Whole-faculty study groups: A powerful way to change schools and enhance learning.* Thousand Oaks, CA: Corwin.

Nagy, W. E., & Scott, J. A. (2000). Vocabulary processes. In M. L. Kamil, P. Mosenthal, P. D. Pearson, & R. Barr (Eds.), *Handbook of reading research: Vol. 3* (pp. 269–284). Mahwah, NJ: Erlbaum.

National Association for the Education of Young Children & National Association of Early Childhood Specialists in State Departments of Education. (2002). *Early learning standards: Creating the conditions for success.* Washington, DC: NAEYC.

National Association for the Education of Young Children & National Association of Early Childhood Specialists in State Departments of Education. (2003). *Early childhood curriculum, child assessment and program evaluation: Building an accountable and effective system for children birth through age eight. A joint position statement of NAEYC and NAECS/SDE.* Washington, DC: NAEYC. Online: http://www.naeyc.org/about/positions/cape.asp

National Board for Professional Teaching Standards. (2001). *Early childhood generalist standards* (2nd ed.). Arlington, VA: Author.

National Center for Education and the Economy. (2001). *New standards: Speaking and listening.* Washington, DC: Author.

National Head Start Summer Teacher Education Program (S.T.E.P.). (2002). *Teachers' manual.* Washington, DC: U.S. Department of Health and Human Services.

National Institute for Child Health and Human Development, Early Child Care Research Network. (2005). Pathways to reading: The role of oral language in the transition to reading. *Developmental Psychology, 41,* 428–442.

National Reading Panel. (2000). *A report of the National Reading Panel: Teaching children to read.* Washington, DC: National Institute of Child Health and Human Development.

National Research Council. (2001). *Report of the Committee on Early Childhood Pedagogy Commission on Behavioral and Social Sciences and Education.* Washington, DC: Author.

Neuman, S., & Roskos, K. (2005). The state of state prekindergarten standards. *Early Childhood Research Quarterly, 20,* 125–145.

New Jersey State Department of Education. (2004). *Preschool teaching and learning expectations: Standards of quality.* Retrieved November 20, 2005, from http://www.nj.gov/njded/ece/expectations/

New York State Education Department & The State University of New York. (n.d.). *Early literacy guidance: Prekindergarten–grade 3.* Retrieved November 20, 2005 from http://www.emsc.nysed.gov/ciai/ela/early.pdf.

Paris, S., Wasik, B., & Turner, J. (1991). The development of strategic readers. In R. Barr, M. Kamil, P. Mosenthal, & P. D. Pearson (Eds.), *Handbook of reading research; Vol. 2* (pp. 609–640). New York: Longman.

Piaget, J. (1926). *The language and thought of the child.* London: Routledge & Kegan Paul.

RAND Reading Study Group. (2002). *Reading for understanding: Toward an R & D program in reading comprehension.* Santa Monica, CA: RAND Corporation.

Rueda, R., & Garcia, G. E. (2002). Topic 9: How do I teach reading to English language learners? In S. Neuman, S. Stahl, N. Duke, P. D. Pearson, S. Paris, B. M. Taylor, et al. (Eds.), *Teaching every child to read: Frequently asked questions* (pp. 1–6). Ann Arbor, MI: Center for the Improvement of Early Reading Achievement.

Schickedanz, J. A., & Casburge, R. M. (2004). *Writing in preschool: Learning to orchestrate meaning and marks.* Newark, DE: IRA.

Seefeldt, C. (2005). *How to work with standards in the early childhood classroom.* New York: Teachers College Press.

Shonkoff, J. P., & Phillips, D. A. (Eds.). (2000). *From neurons to neighborhoods: The science of early childhood development.* Washington, DC: National Academy Press.

Shore, R., Bodrova, E., & Leong, D. (2004). Child outcome standards in pre–K programs: What are standards; what is needed to make them work? *Preschool Policy Matters* (No. 5). New Brunswick, NJ: NIEER.

Skinner, B. F. (1974). *About behaviorism.* New York: Knopf.

Snow, C. E., Barnes, W. S., Chandler, J., Goodman, J. F., & Hemphill, L. (1991). *Unfulfilled expectations: Home and school influences on literacy.* Cambridge, MA: Harvard University Press.

Snow, C. E., Burns, M. S., & Griffin, P. (Eds.). (1998). *Preventing reading difficulties in young children.* Washington, DC: National Academy Press.

Sprira, E. G., Bracken, S. S., & Fischel, J. E. (2005). Predicting improvement after first-grade reading difficulties: The effects of oral language, emergent literacy, and behavior skills. *Developmental Psychology, 41,* 225–234.

Storch, S., & Whitehurst, G. (2002). Oral language and code-related precursors to reading: Evidence from a longitudinal structural model. *Developmental Psychology, 38,* 934–947.

St. Pierre, R. G., & Layzer, J. I. (1998). Improving the life chances of children in poverty: Assumptions and what we have learned. *Social Policy Report, 12*(4), 1–25.

Strickland, D. (1988). Some tips for using big books. *The Reading Teacher, 41,* 966–967.

Strickland, D. S. (2001). Early intervention for African American children considered to be at risk. In S. B. Neuman & D. K. Dickinson (Eds.), *Handbook of early literacy research* (pp. 322–332). New York: Guilford.

Strickland, D. S. (2004). Literacy in early childhood education: The search for balance. *Children & Families, 18,* 24–31.

Strickland, D. S., & Barnett, W. S. (2003). Literacy interventions for preschool children considered at risk: Implications for curriculum, professional development, and parent involvement. In C. Fairbanks, J. Worthy, B. Maloch, J. V. Hoffman, & D. Schallert (Eds.), *52nd yearbook of the National Reading Conference* (pp. 104–116). Oak Creek, WI: National Reading Conference.

Strickland, D. S., Ganske, K., & Monroe, J. K. (2002). *Supporting struggling readers and writers: Strategies for classroom intervention 3–6.* Portland, ME: Stenhouse.

Strickland, D. S., & Kamil, M. (2004). *Improving reading achievement through professional development.* Norwood, MA: Christopher-Gordon.

Strickland, D. S., & Riley-Ayers, S. (2006). *Early literacy: Policy and practice in the preschool years.* New Brunswick, NJ: NIEER.

Strickland, D. S., & Schickedanz, J. A. (2004). *Learning about print in preschool: Working with letters, words, and beginning links with phonemic awareness.* Newark, DE: IRA.

Strickland, D. S., & Shanahan, T. (2004). Laying the groundwork for literacy. *Educational Leadership, 61,* 74–77.

Suarez-Orozco, M. M. (2001). Globalization, immigration, and education: The research agenda. *Harvard Educational Review, 71,* 345–365.

Tabors, P. O., Snow, C. E., & Dickinson, D. K. (2001). Homes and schools together: Supporting language and literacy development. In D. K. Dickinson & P. O. Tabors (Eds.), *Beginning literacy with language: Young children learning at home and school* (pp. 313–334). Baltimore, MD: Brookes.

Teachers of English to Speakers of Other Languages. (1997). *ESL standards for pre-K–12 students.* Arlington, VA. Author.

Teale, W. H., & Sulzby, E. (1989). Emergent literacy: New perspectives. In D. S. Strickland & L. M. Morrow (Eds.), *Emerging literacy: Young children learn to read and write* (pp. 1–15). Newark, DE: IRA.

U.S. Census Bureau. (2003). *United States Department of Commerce News.* Washington, DC. Retrieved July 24, 2003, from http://www.census.gov/Press-Release/www/2003/cb03-100.html

U.S. Department of Education, Office of Educational Research and Improvement. (1996). *Family literacy: Directions in research and implications for practice.* Washington, DC: Author.

U.S. Department of Health and Human Services, Office of the Assistant Secretary for Planning and Evaluation. (2003). *Strengthening Head Start: What the evidence shows.* Washington, DC: Author.

Vukelich, C. (2004). In search of highly qualified early childhood classroom literacy teachers. *The Reading Teacher, 58,* 95–100.

Vygotsky, L. (1962). *Thought and language.* New York: Wiley.

Wells, G. (1985). Preschool literacy-related activities and success in school. In D. R. Olson, N. Torrance, & A. Hildyard (Eds.), *Literacy, language and learning: The nature and consequences of reading and writing* (pp. 229–255). New York: Cambridge University Press.

Index

About the Authors

Dorothy S. Strickland, Ph.D., is the Samuel DeWitt Proctor Professor of Education at Rutgers, the State University of New Jersey, and a distinguished fellow at the National Institute for Early Education Research at Rutgers. A former classroom teacher, reading consultant, and learning disabilities specialist, she is a past president of both the International Reading Association and the IRA Reading Hall of Fame. She received IRA's Outstanding Teacher Educator of Reading Award, the National Council of Teachers of English Award as Outstanding Educator in the Language Arts, and the National-Louis University Ferguson Award for Outstanding Contributions to Early Childhood Education. She was a member of the panels that produced *Becoming a Nation of Readers, Preventing Reading Difficulties in Young Children, The RAND Report, Reading for Understanding,* and the *National Early Literacy Panel.* Her latest publications include *Learning about Print in Preschool Settings* and *Improving Reading Achievement Through Professional Development.*

Shannon Riley-Ayers, Ph.D., is an Assistant Research Professor at the National Institute for Early Education Research at Rutgers University. Before her work at NIEER, she was instrumental in developing and implementing the New Jersey Early Literacy Initiative while co-directing the Office of Early Literacy at the Department of Education. She is a certified teacher and reading specialist and has several years' experience in the classrooms of public schools. Her work has also included teaching preservice teachers and teachers earning their master's degree. She holds an M.Ed. in language and literacy and a Ph.D. in educational psychology from The Pennsylvania State University. She is co-author (with Dorothy Strickland) of the policy brief *Early Literacy: Policy and Practice in the Preschool Years.*